C000109176

Once A Malim Sahib

Once A Malim Sahib

The Memoirs of a Deck Officer

Ian Milner

Librario

Published by
Librario Publishing Ltd.

ISBN : 978-1906775100

Copies can be ordered from retail
or via the internet at :

www.librario.com

or from :

Brough House
Milton Brodie
Kinloss
Morayshire
IV36 2UA

Tel / Fax : 01343 850178

Cover design and layout by Steven James
www.chimeracreations.co.uk

Printed and bound in Great Britain by
4edge Ltd, Hockley. www.4edge.co.uk

© 2010 Ian Milner

The Author has asserted his moral right to be
identified as the Author of this Work. No part of this book
may be reproduced, stored in a retrieval system, or transmitted
by any means, electronic, mechanical, photocopying, recording,
or otherwise, without permission from the author.

Dedication

Merchant Navy Veterans Badge

This book is dedicated to the men and women of the Merchant Navy past and present whose loyalty and commitment always ensured that Britain's vital supply lines were maintained during hostilities, and that the armed services were fully supported wherever required. I count myself privileged to have been able to serve with them at that time.

The Merchant Navy Veterans Badge is awarded to those who were directly involved in military operations in support of the armed services. The administration of the scheme is shared by the Merchant Navy Association, and the Federation of Merchant Mariners.

CONTENTS

Self Portrait Sketch

Foreword
by Richard Boardman

Compared with my own rather dull apprenticeship, Ian Milner's was rich in experience. Although his book is sub-titled *The Memoirs of a Deck Officer,* it is easy in reading it to forget that Milner was extraordinarily fortunate in being seconded from the British India Steam Navigation Company while still 'doing his time' and before he was, at least in the eyes of the Board of Trade, an officer proper.

Milner went to sea early in 1945 in the last months of the Second World War by which time the Allies had the upper hand at sea. As a salutary reminder that the war at sea went the full distance, he was torpedoed on his first voyage in the S.S. *Neuralia.* I had a personal interest in the fate of this ship because my own father, when a sixth-form school-boy, had undertaken an educational cruise to the Baltic and recalled her for the spotlessness of her decks from which he observed the antics of the Nazi brown-shirts on the banks of the Kiel Canal.

Repatriated, Milner was appointed to the *Gurna.* He must have impressed his lords and masters sufficiently, for on arrival at Bombay he was 'loaned' to the Admiralty Salvage Service. Aboard the salvage tug *Salviola,* as an uncertificated officer, he learned of the attraction and satisfaction of working in a small vessel. The *Salviola* was engaged in the Persian Gulf, clearing up the refuse of war. Many ports were as yet untouched by the boom in oil exports and retained some of the characteristics of an earlier age; features which Milner recognises in this well wrought account of salvage work at a time when it remained relatively unsophisticated.

Milner returned to British India but, in the end, decided not to stay at sea; for a young man of obvious ability that was a pity. Nevertheless, his recollections of his youth are a timely reminder of what we once were as a seafaring nation.

R.M.W.
2010

Chapter One

In at the Deep End

Great expectations . . .

When I climbed the gangway of the *TSS Neuralia* in London's Royal Albert Dock in January 1945 wearing my brand new uniform, and reported for duty as a deck officer cadet, I didn't expect to be scrambling off again . . . at night . . . down a rope only four months later. I was unprepared, so to speak, when the alarm sounding 'Abandon ship!' shattered my sleep and I found myself struggling to get dressed against the steeply listing deck at 2am on 1st May.

As a veteran troopship, *Neuralia* had never been far from the action during the war periods of her thirty-year career. She had recently landed troops in Tripoli, Taranto and Naples and lain off the Normandy beaches for the *D-Day* landings. This was, of course, all before I joined her, but as my first ship she has always claimed a special place in my affections.

TSS Neuralia looking elegant in peace time livery. © *NMM*

For me, it was a four month 'taster' for this whole new world into which I had so eagerly ventured. The convoys, U-boat scares, missing escort, minor fire and sabotage – all before we reached Gibraltar – were par for the course in those days, I suppose.

This was followed by hectic activity and excitement when we reached the Eastern Mediterranean, our new field of operations, including the accidental ramming of a tug in Alexandria; getting both anchors fouled while moored in Port Said; and tearing our mooring bollards from the badly damaged quay in Piraeus (Port of Athens). Then we were nearly overrun while returning some rather fierce Greek partisans, before finally getting into allegiance problems with the Yugoslav resistance fighters.

To give us a fighting chance to defend ourselves in the battle against the dive bombers and U-boats, we had been generously equipped with a surprisingly impressive armament manned by a detachment of 'D.E.M.S.'* gunners.

It included two Twelve Pounders on the 'fo'c'sle' (deck at the bow), four 'Bofors' anti-aircraft guns on the boat deck and eight rapid firing 'Oerlikons' which carried their gunners through an exciting 360 degree free swing (until 'stops' were fitted to save them raking the bridge of their own ship with fire as they followed the diving plane in the heat of the chase).

To top all this off, we had a huge 4.7 inch gun mounted right aft on top of the isolation ward of our hospital. This would certainly have taken the mind of any unfortunate inmate off his medical problems when the gun was fired.

*Defensive Equipment Merchant Ships-manned by the Royal Maritime Regiment and other servicemen volunteers.

But to get back to the events of 1ˢᵗ May and our rude awakening . . . we had been rounding the 'heel' of Italy on passage from Split in Yugoslavia to Taranto in the bay of Taranto, Southern Italy, and preparing to take on board a full complement of German prisoners. Perhaps surprisingly, German prisoners were generally greeted with enthusiasm for more than the obvious reason. We always found that their routine left the ship cleaner and sweeter than from any other troops. This contrasted somewhat with the 'British Pongo' who took great pride in his ability to achieve a full body wash with the aid of a single damp sponge (learned undoubtedly from experience during the desert campaigns).

Shock can do very strange things to the human mind – especially when it occurs during deep sleep. Getting hastily dressed for reporting to my life-boat station, I remember carefully putting away my No. 1 uniform 'so that it would not get messed up in the lifeboat', and getting into my working uniform. One man was seen frantically going through a stack of life jackets on the promenade deck. When challenged he insisted that he 'had to find the one with his name on'!

I think it was our electrician who got as far as tying the bow tie from his mess kit from the previous night, before suddenly realizing the urgency of his situation and bolting for safety without waiting to put on his trousers.

More of a problem was caused by one of the gunners. He had 'frozen' with vertigo and was clinging to the top of one of the knotted ropes down which he had to drop to reach the lifeboat which was tossing about in the water some fifty feet below. It took time and patience (which were both in short supply at the time) to 'un-stick' him and get him safely down into the boat. But he got there in the end. I remember feeling more excitement than fear, no doubt due to adrenalin-fed immortality of youth, as I teamed up with our

The boat deck on the Neuralia.

Quartermaster and we moved along the boat deck lowering the remaining boats between us. Fortunately in this period of apparent calm our stricken ship seemed almost to have paused to let us get safely away as she settled down slowly in the water.

When it seemed that all the useable boats on our side of the ship had been lowered, we went back to our own boat station and made our way down into our boat. There we found, as we slowly made out the scene in the darkness, that we had landed on a heap of shivering half dressed members of the crew lying in the bottom of the wildly rearing and plunging boat. It was at this point that thanks to the pleadings of a shivering near naked body that reared up in front of me on my arrival, I was 'persuaded' to part with my favourite white woollen polo necked sweater that I had hastily tied round my neck as I left my cabin. Needless to say, that was the last I saw of it. The enormity of my sacrifice was slow to hit me as I contemplated what a large proportion of my few remaining possessions this represented.

Whilst still tethered to the ship in the choppy sea conditions, the lifeboat was repeatedly smashed against the hull by the waves, damaging the port side timber gunwale (which would prevent us rigging the oars on that side). But all that paled into insignificance when we realised that there was to be no rapid departure for us as the 'for'd fall block' had jammed on the hoisting hook in the lifeboat preventing us from disengaging from the sinking ship at all.

Climbing down into the bow compartment of the boat was tricky as the trough of each wave jerked the 'fall block' up as it took the weight of the boat. I could only try to release the hook when the boat rose again on the next wave. My efforts were in vain. Cutting the ropes was our only hope. My clasp knife seemed to make painfully slow progress on these heavy ropes jerking away on every wave but at last we had cut enough to pull free. By this time I was feeling pretty queasy and exhausted. As efforts to start the engine had failed, and we were unable to row other than in circles, we became resigned to the fact that for the time being we were reduced to drifting. Thus when dawn broke at about 5.30am we were still close enough to watch *Neuralia's* final moments in the half light. She settled by the stern, raised her bow high in the air and after hesitating for a few moments finally agreed to slip quietly below the surface. It was at that point that I realized that putting my No. 1 uniform away in my wardrobe to keep it clean had not been such a great idea.

My initial thoughts in the lifeboat were for my family who, no doubt, would be worried to hear that I was missing. In the event, they were spared any anxiety as they had heard nothing of the ship's loss. I was allowed to send a brief message reassuring them that I was still all right, but as they had no idea that anything untoward had happened, simply thought 'Oh that's good, Ian's OK', as I later discovered.

Later that day we were spotted by a passing Italian 'coaster', thankfully undeterred by the presence of mines and it was then only a matter of time before rescue seemed inevitable. Ironically, we were all soon to be brought back to life again. This occurred because we weren't able to bring our boat alongside the coaster (which was incidentally in ballast and therefore high out of the water), so they had gradually to manoeuvre alongside us. Murphy's Law ensured that as they came close, their engine-room condenser cooling water discharge, high above us, which was hurling out a deluge of hot waters, slowly raked us from stem to stern giving us all a hot shower which we were certainly not expecting. Our evacuation from the boat developed a new impetus, as our energies were quickly revived from our somewhat weary and lethargic state.

Shortly we were to be landed at Gallipoli (in Italy) and after a check up at the military hospital in Taranto we were passed through a military transit camp so that we could draw essential kit to get us home. We embarked on the troop ship *Samaria,* spending VE day at Malta before transferring to the MV *Georgic* in Naples for the voyage home to Liverpool. The *Georgic* had herself survived being bombed and burnt out at Suez in 1941, then remarkably she was salvaged, towed to India and given an amazing nine month refit which got her back into service again. Her very eventful past was in evidence below decks where you were greeted by the badly buckled plating of the accommodation. Clearly, the distortion caused by the heat of the fire that had enveloped her could not be disguised by the new paintwork of the quick refit she was given.

We sailed from Naples on 12th May and settled down to enjoy a lazy run home making the most of our unplanned cruise.

As 'survivors' being repatriated in just what we stood up in, we set foot on British soil to find that we qualified for assistance from the 'Shipwrecked Mariners' Society' (reminding us rather starkly of our true status). But it did provide us with rail tickets home from Liverpool which were, nonetheless, gratefully received.

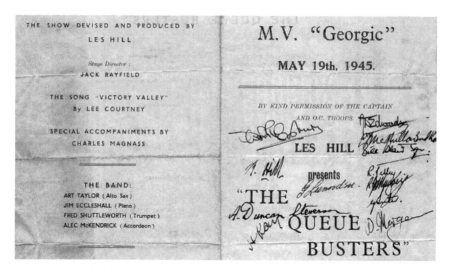

THE SHOW DEVISED AND PRODUCED BY
LES HILL

Stage Director :
JACK RAYFIELD

THE SONG "VICTORY VALLEY"
By LEE COURTNEY

SPECIAL ACCOMPANIMENTS BY
CHARLES MAGNASS

THE BAND:
ART TAYLOR (Alto Sax)
JIM ECCLESHALL (Piano)
FRED SHUTTLEWORTH (Trumpet)
ALEC McKENDRICK (Accordeon)

M.V. "Georgic"

MAY 19th, 1945.

BY KIND PERMISSION OF THE CAPTAIN
AND O.C. TROOPS.

LES HILL

presents

"THE QUEUE BUSTERS"

Ship's Concert Programme that we autographed to mark our survival.

So three weeks after abandoning ship, I was home in Warwickshire. As I walked down the path, with my small bag of belongings and pushed open the door, my mother looked up from what she was doing in the kitchen.

"Oh it's you, is it Ian? I wondered why the dog was so restless," she said, having known nothing of my recent experiences. It was good to be part of home life again, and felt almost as though nothing had happened. But what a story I had to tell. In some extraordinary way it felt like an entirely satisfactory conclusion to my first venture, and one that gave me what I craved most – experience and the knowledge that I was no longer a 'greenhorn'.

I wondered what my next ship would hold in store. But whatever it might be, it was unlikely to be more testing than my first, especially as I now had the benefit of my newly acquired confidence, a priceless legacy from dear old *Neuralia*.

At the start of the war, my company, the British India Steam Navigation Co. owned the largest fleet of merchant ships in the world. A total of forty-six ships were sunk by enemy action during the hostilities. *Neuralia* bowed out at number forty-five. It was an untimely end after thirty-three years of faithful service, going down just days before VE Day.

As I contemplated my first spell at sea since signing my Indentures (which bound me to serve the Company for four years in return for my training and keep), I felt fairly satisfied that I had successfully stepped out of civilian life straight onto my first ship. With no prior training, I had possessed simply a trunk full of kit purchased by my devoted parents and a rough and ready knowledge of what life at sea would be all about. Most of this had been gleaned from the pen of Percy F Westerman with whose well-researched sea stories I had grown up. Then with barely time to get used to the routine of well-ordered life on board ship, we had left our London dockside to join a series of convoys en route for the Mediterranean.

I had never been in any doubt that I would go to sea; it had always seemed to me the natural thing to do. When I took my place on the bridge for the first time it was more a case of finding *where* things were than discovering *what* they were. *Neuralia* had taught me to value and rely on my shipmates as we shared the experience, taking everything in our stride no matter how unexpected.

A typical convoy gathering.

Convoys were an amazing achievement of co-operation by a generally motley collection of ships varying from slick liners to the battered tramp ships. The Navy's escort ships, rather like sheep dogs, rounded up the stragglers as they all struggled to maintain the speed set by the Commodore but dictated by the slowest ship (which was probably steaming flat out and hoping that nothing would blow in the engine room). 'Keeping a sharp look-out' took on a new meaning as we all struggled to maintain our positions relative to our neighbours, always looking for torpedo tracks heading our way, not to mention the chance of an air attack.

All this became more complicated, not to say hazardous, when fog descended. The danger then came from each other rather than the enemy and often took us by surprise when it finally lifted and it was evident that a quiet re-shuffle of the pack had taken place without anyone needing a change of underwear.

This situation led to the introduction of a cunning device, which like many of the ingenious ideas that were put into practice in the interests of survival, always maintained an almost home-made appeal. This was the 'fog buoy', a wooden, coffin-like box about a metre long which was trailed by the ships at a fixed distance behind them. This enabled the helmsman of the following vessel to spot a tall plume of spray scooped up by the design of the box as it was hauled through the water). What's more, the distance between ships could be adjusted by lengthening or shortening the towing line. Thus everyone was able to maintain their proper position even though the ship ahead was herself buried in the fog. I found this somehow very practical and reassuring.

An archive shot of Neuralia in wartime style. © NMM

On leaving the protection of the convoy we made our first stop at the Azores, where we were to pick up our own personal escort vessel before proceeding to Gibraltar as there was known to be a U-boat operating in the area. When our escort finally arrived we were surprised to find it to be in the 'motor launch' class, which we could have blown clean out of the water with one broadside from our own armament, but I suppose that really wasn't the point as they were fast, agile, and carried depth charges.

And so it was that we made it into the Med. without serious mishap. Although, there was an incident one night while we were dodging the U-boats when the boat-launching floodlights were mysteriously turned on making us a well-illuminated target. We never did find the saboteur responsible.

Gibraltar was our first stop, then Algiers with its fascinating Kasbah and what seemed to us strangely bright lights boasting its neutrality. By now I had settled into my routine on board and felt completely in my element. Shipmates in these conditions soon become close friends and although wartime life at sea has been described as 'long periods of boredom punctuated by moments of extreme danger', boredom was never a problem for us.

I well remember one night as we junior officers sat at our dinner table in the main saloon, at a respectful distance from the Captain's table, our 3rd Radio Operator felt the sudden urge to reveal his innermost feelings undeterred by the proximity of our fellow diners. His heavy Irish brogue, spotty face and tousled hair were somehow untamed by his smart uniform. Suddenly he pointed to the Captain who was sitting with the six young members of the Nursing Yeomanry that we happened to be carrying, and proclaimed:

"There's that Old B*****d, sixty if he's a day, with six young Fannys round him, and here am I twenty-one and dying of masturbation!" As luck would have it, this coincided with a lull in the general level of conversation and as the ensuing roars of laughter showed, everyone seemed to have got the message. His scarlet face left no doubt as to who was the originator of the outburst and he never really lived it down.

For a while we were engaged in shuttling between Alexandria and Piraeus repatriating members of the Greek freedom fighters E.L.A.S. and E.A.M. back to their recently liberated country, and it was on one of these arrivals in Piraeus that we seemed to come unstuck. We moored with one anchor off the bow and two stern lines onto bollards on the stone quay behind us, and had just stood down from the bridge and started to relax when 'Stations for leaving port!' was sounded. Incredulous at first, we soon found that it was for real as our stern lines had both carried away, by simply pulling the cast iron bollards out from the masonry and dumping them in the dock. Evidently the damage done to the dockside during the German retreat had weakened the whole structure and the strong offshore wind had proved too much for the bollards to hold.

'Do not proceed to sea' came the signal from Port Control as we struggled to free our stern lines without wrapping the mooring wires round our starboard propeller. Unable for this reason to use our engines, we sent an urgent request for tugs, but failed to get an acknowledgement, just '*Do not proceed to sea, you should await orders*'. In desperation our signal lamp responded with '*All shore lines carried away please send tugs urgently*'. Still no acknowledgement, so we went on repeating our signal in the hope of some response.

Suddenly there appeared a veritable armada of tugs heading for us. Apparently each of our many requests had been acted upon and in no time at all we had a forest of masts all along our starboard side, rather like a fishing fleet in port. To add to the suspense, during the struggle, our local pilot appeared to put the helm over the wrong way after getting the propeller clear of the submerged mooring wires so that we seemed certain to be back in trouble again. The Captain exploded in fury.

"You've done it again pilot! Get off my bridge you garlic eating sod!" whereupon the man promptly obliged and waited patiently under the bridge while we carefully unhitched ourselves again. Apologies followed later as we anchored safely outside the harbour and I have to say, I thought he took it all remarkably well, leaving us to sort ourselves out with Port Control.

The more northern ports of Volos and Kavalla also presented interesting berthing problems as they struggled back to normality after the occupation and German retreat. Kavalla left us with a sombre image of extermination camps and massive incinerators around which the smell of fear and death lingered on.

Consequently our orders to make the next trip from Alexandria to Split, on the Adriatic coast of Yugoslavia, carrying returning refugees was welcomed as an altogether more cheerful assignment. It is fair to say that we were generally concentrating on the job in hand rather than studying the political manoeuvring of the peoples around us, and therefore we were shocked when the cabins we offered to the pregnant, the young mums, the sick and infirm (who we felt might have had problems with our trooping hammocks) were rejected on the grounds that as they couldn't all have cabins, none of them would be allowed to use them. So they stood empty for the trip.

This, we were told, was what Communism was all about, nevertheless we still built up good relations with our passengers who entertained us with traditional singing and folk dancing and presented us with a beautiful silk flag. This, although similar to the Yugoslavian flag in our signal locker, had a red and gold star in the centre which ours did not. Nevertheless it seemed churlish not to hoist the silk flag as our courtesy ensign as is customary on entering territorial waters. We were, however, somewhat surprised at the scale of celebration that met us as we neared our destination, and we did notice that flags flying ashore which had *no* star seemed to come quietly down. The surprise ended when we learned that we were inadvertently signalling we had joined the rebels and were the largest ship to have done so. Maybe it was time to move on. Certainly the disappearance of our lovely young interpreter for apparently getting too friendly with us and the bullet holes in our decks added to our concerns. When we saw pathetic prisoners of war ashore, carrying railway lines on their shoulders, clad in rags and many without boots, we were encouraged to be on our ill-fated way.

This was how it came about that we were steaming into the Gulf of Taranto on the night of 2nd May concentrating on our next task: the collection of 1,500 German prisoners. Their treatment at the hands of the British troops recently assigned to us would contrast sharply with the scenes witnessed in Split. These troops, on guard duty, had been requested after our unfortunate brush with the Greek resistance fighters who decided to help themselves to our stores by cutting off the bridge from the crew during the passage. This had left us feeling a bit vulnerable.

Chapter Two

SS Gurna,
My New Home

SS Gurna

Orders to join my next ship arrived on 20th June 1945. Lying in King George V Dock in London, she proved to be a First World War Standard Cargo ship with accommodation for 24 passengers converted from the upper decks of the cargo hold. She had been used as a mine depot ship during the hostilities, able to carry 2,000 mines. Not the most popular neighbour in convoys but luckily the size of the bang was never ultimately put to the test. We were to load bulk cement at Purfleet before heading for East Africa.

Leaving Tilbury on 26th July we were past Gibraltar by 1st August and then on to Port Said where for my first time I experienced the complex rituals of negotiating the Suez Canal at night. The channel was marked by buoys carrying reflectors which picked up the beam of the huge search light that was hoisted onto our bows so that we could proceed through the night guided by our pilot, one of an elite multinational band.

Mombasa was definitely to my liking, especially as our Captain had decided that we young sprogetts should leave the ship while it was enveloped in a thick cloud of cement dust during unloading. We were accommodated at the Officers' Club in mud-type huts where it was obviously considered important to take precautions against the predators. Hence the bowls of water that the bed legs stood in (to deter the non-swimming crawlies); the strip of hessian suspended above the beds (to catch the snakes that dropped out of the thatch); and the bars in the windows (to keep out the light fingered monkeys). All were designed to give that ultimate peace of mind that a simple mosquito net might struggle to provide.

During a brief but pleasant spell in Tanga, we cadets crewed for the local agent on his racing yacht and sailed out to the coral reef with a cargo of cold chicken and colder beer. Life in peacetime East Africa seemed good to us. Then we proceeded on to the romantic sounding Zanzibar, and Dar es Salaam before finishing our passage south at Durban. A cargo ship has a definite advantage over passenger ships with their rapid turnaround – we were able to see much more of the places we visited.

It was whilst in Durban that I found myself working on a farm. It was my own farm situated on the 'after well' deck. I had twenty-five South African sheep, six prize bulls and a cow with a three-week-old bull calf, Bambi. Perhaps I should explain. On 15th October we came back from the Durban coaling berth to P shed to embark passengers and livestock. After emerging from the saloon and breakfast, I went off to receive passengers' baggage and stow it away. I had just started when the Mate sent for me. I found him on the 'after well' deck surrounded by bales of straw and grass, and bags of oats. Bulls were being led into stalls, and sheep (the most enormous I've ever seen) being led into hastily-constructed pens.

"These are all yours now Milner," he said, "find out as much as you can and get organised." And that was that. I looked dubiously at the large and ferocious bull that was being pushed protesting into its stall by four men; at the ever-growing stack of grasses and hay, bags and bales; and the mass of huge fluffy woollen backs all but filling the pens. I swallowed hard. Feverishly, I began finding out about the stock, their food and bedding. I glanced again at the brief slip of feeding instructions which had been quietly put into my hand. The farmer chap began casually pointing out the different kinds of grass, foods and their uses, the value of each sheep and how the bulls were not *just* bulls but valuable prize bulls. I broke into a cold sweat. Finally, he gave instructions on the welfare of the calf and was gone.

I surveyed the scene. All the livestock was on board but their food was all over the place. I stowed the grain and the meal in our old ammunition stores on the poop deck. The bales of grass and stuff soon formed a hay stack on top of No. 5 hatch. The next day, the calf was sick from having too much of his mother's milk and had to be tied up. This meant milking the cow to take up the surplus. Luckily, I found that two of the Kalassis crew had farm experience in their own country, India. I was confidently able to promise a daily fresh milk supply to the saloon probably for the first time in the ship's history.

The daily chore of mucking out the bulls and cow also took on unexpected significance as I found to my astonishment that my Kalassi farm hands had discarded the shovels I'd provided on 'religious grounds'. Being Hindus, they considered the animals to be sacred, so that their by-products could only be removed with yes, their bare hands. I was proudly able to announce to my colleagues on the bridge that we were probably the only ship in the fleet that included in its daily routine, the disposal of bullshit by the handful over the side. A rare distinction we all agreed.

A Kalassi from my sketchbook.

It became clear that the Mate was unimpressed that all my beasts were healthy, happy and as natural as circumstances permitted. He heavily criticised the state of the bulls describing them as looking scruffy and unkempt with the odd tick visible. I was cut to the quick and resolved to strike back as we approached our destination, Mombasa.

Starting with the friendliest bull I climbed into its stall armed with a big scrubbing brush and started brushing its coat, only to find that he loved it and became even more docile. This encouraged me to advance up the line to the ferocious, evil looking one at the end. Luckily it worked. But whilst he was OK when the brush was in contact, as soon as you stopped he reverted to his normal angry state, and you were there at your peril.

I then concentrated on their heads, and soon had all their horns highly polished and quite splendid. To add the finishing touch, I used the Quartermaster's beeswax to tame their long whiskers into impressive moustaches and goatees, and neatly parted their hair over their horns. The effect was stunning. They all looked very distinguished and certainly not at all scruffy.

I don't know who was the most shocked, the Mate or the farmer who came to take delivery, both appeared lost for words. But luckily good humour prevailed and I got away with a ticking off for over-enthusiasm. So the smart bulls were soon on their way to pastures new, so to speak, and I was able to return to more normal cargo handling. This episode served to remind me that as a merchant seaman I was expected to take pretty much any human activity in my stride – from sewing to childbirth, via animal husbandry. I was to be reminded of this on a later voyage when I got to know the less attractive habits of monkeys, pregnant race horses and even a young leopard (to name but a few).

From Mombasa we crossed to Bombay where after a couple of weeks discharging and loading cargo we sailed on 19th November for Abadan at the top of the Persian Gulf before heading back to London and the retirement of our Captain. It was not long after leaving Bombay however that the Captain, who had joined us in Port Said to go home, collapsed whilst talking to some passengers on the deck. Doc called me to give him a hand and we applied artificial respiration with various heart stimulants for about half an hour. But we were forced eventually to accept that he was a gonner. As he had a known heart condition, Doc was in no doubt as to cause of death.

On reporting this to the Mate, I discovered him to be as white as a sheet and so shocked that he was quite unable to give us any help. So it was left to

Doc, the other cadet and me to carry the Captain into his day cabin, where we laid him on the table ready to be prepared for the burial process the next day.

I was to secure the heavy iron fire bars to the body and oversee the Quartermaster sewing up the canvas, but I didn't realise just how harrowing this would prove to be. The high temperature we were experiencing had a dramatic effect on the body overnight and when we went in to the half-lit cabin the next morning, we were shocked to find his skin black with ants and starting noticeably to decompose. Undaunted however, we arranged the fire bars on either side and passed the cordage under and around him. I was so determined that the bars would not be able to break away when the body hit the water forty feet below leaving him floating in our wake, that I put my foot against his side and heaved the lashing tight with all my might.

What happened then was so eerie that the Quartermaster bolted and nothing could persuade him to come back. For, unmistakably, the corpse had uttered a long guttural moan. Impossible I told myself – and yet he had. My first reaction was to try resuscitation but I rapidly abandoned this when it was obvious that he was decomposing quite fast in the heat. Gradually, it dawned on me that it must have been my desperate tightening of the lashing around the bars that had squeezed his chest, sharply expelling the air from his lungs through his windpipe and past his vocal cords which still worked.

Unfortunately, I was unable to convince the Indian Quartermaster of my simple explanation and I don't think he ever quite recovered.

Nothing much could stop us now. We two cadets had to finish the job as securely and as quickly as possible. We wrapped the body in best canvas, sewing it up with the last stitch through the nose (as is traditional but not very easy). Our troubles didn't stop there, however, as we discovered when we came to transfer the body down onto the fore deck for the burial ceremony.

We had, of course, placed him on a stretcher. Carrying this out on deck was fairly straightforward with enough hands (even with the considerable extra weight of the iron bars). It was only when we came to negotiate the near vertical accommodation ladder down on to the promenade deck that things started to get a bit out of hand.

To say those next few minutes were not in the finest traditions of a solemn and dignified funeral ceremony would, I fear, be an understatement. There were certainly times when it appeared likely he would be making a premature departure. As the stretcher inclined more and more to the rake of the steps, his urge to go on ahead became almost irresistible. Somehow, however, with much sweating and heaving we got him down to the main deck where, at last, he was placed on a greased timber hatch cover under a red ensign poised for committing to the deep.

Fortunately, none of this detracted from the poignancy of the simple service read by our Mate whose hands were still visibly shaking with emotion. After a heartfelt verse of *'Those in Peril'*, the moment came. We raised the end of the hatch cover and the canvas-covered form slid silently overboard from beneath the Ensign. I watched with trepidation to see what would happen when it struck the water but thankfully the lashings held and it entered cleanly and carried on down to Davy Jones's Locker. What a relief. Everyone seemed able to relax at last. And as we happened to have a representative of the owners as a passenger, he was able to authorise us to carry on and not turn back, so it was temporary promotion all round.

We steamed on up the Persian Gulf without further drama until we picked up our pilot on entering the Shatt Al Arab River and glided in pitch darkness between banks of date palms, mud huts, moored dhows and canoes. We passed the city-like oil refinery at Abadan, brilliantly ablaze with shafts of flames, myriads of light and served by its line of tankers. We reached Koramshahr, home of the Iranian Navy, where we anchored and discharged part of our cargo. I didn't know then how soon I was destined to return to the naval base on quite a different mission. I was to spend nine months of my young life struggling to wrestle a sunken vessel from the all-pervading river mud that had claimed it.

Moving on to Basra, we discharged the remainder of our cargo and loaded dates for home. It was not long before we found ourselves involved with quite a different sort of 'date'. We discovered that our new passenger list held an Ambassador and his entire secretarial entourage. Most of these were young and most definitely female, albeit only French speaking.

For whatever reason, life on board had inevitably been different after the sad episode of our Captain's untimely death, but this was to add quite another dimension – happiness. Crash courses in essential French became a must although it was made more difficult by having to use Urdu as our 'second language' in order to communicate with our Indian crew.

Incidentally, we 'Deck Officers' translated in Urdu to *'Malim Sahibs'*, 'malim' meaning understanding, whereas the Engineers were *'Mistri Sahibs'* which we felt to be a well justified distinction. Little time was lost in getting to know our new friends. It seemed only fair that there were 'enough to go round' and that all ages were nicely matched. A new etiquette was brought in to ensure that a decent interval was allowed to elapse after knocking on a colleague's cabin door before expecting an appearance, a change from our customary habit of barging in.

During the balmy evenings as we made our way up the Red Sea, number two radio operator found that maintaining his normal listening watch tended to interfere with his personal contribution to the ship's *entente cordiale*. Undaunted, he found a very long extension lead for his ear phones which enabled him to maintain his watch from a more congenial position under blankets on deck. This had the advantage that if missing when needed, you could easily trace him by following the lead from the open door of his radio room until you found the appropriate blanket bundle (generally discreetly situated under a nearby lifeboat).

The girls soon got bored during the day, however. My solution was to fit them out in boiler suits and get them working alongside us on deck. This arrangement was eventually approved by the Mate. The work mostly consisted of removing all traces of wartime grey paint from things like the ship's bell and re-stocking the lifeboats.

Life was so good that we seemed to arrive back in the English Channel far too soon, an untypical reaction on glimpsing the white cliffs after being away for a while. It had been an extraordinary voyage. I remember the look of bewilderment on the shipping agent's face as he tried to gather up his passengers to disembark them. They were all much more concerned with fond farewells. He said he had never witnessed a scene like this in the whole of his long career, especially when there seemed to be no one left out.

All too soon we were off again for an uneventful voyage back to the now familiar Bombay where I would come under the control of the local Marine Superintendent who was likely to transfer me to another ship, but this could be on the other side of India, where I could be serving for years on the Indian Coast with no connection to the 'Home Line' plying back westward. It was therefore a worrying place to be, not helped by the seething mass of humanity which seemed to fill every street around the dock area. The chief occupation seemed to be begging assisted by the children whose wretched young bodies had been distorted by the dislocation of their joints to make them more pathetic and entirely dependent on their families. The disturbing attitude to human life prevalent at the time was summed up for me by a Sikh taxi driver who, when told to look out for all the people in the road in front of us, turned round to reassure us by saying:

"Plenty more where they came from Sahib, plenty more where they came from!" as he maintained his speed with horn blaring and foot hard down on accelerator. The effect that all this had on me at the time was only revealed through letters home, where I've noticed that any emotional reaction I had to my experiences brought out a poetic streak, otherwise undisturbed. Thus the prospect of returning to Bombay became:

"... until I again perceive the romantic silhouette of the Taj's dome thrusting up above the maze of mystic spires and minarets, as we glide spellbound to our anchorage and prepare ourselves . . . for the ghastly stench which hits anyone fool enough to venture within a mile of the seething mass of filthy humanity, and vermin infested shacks that we know as Bombay Docks!"

Luckily for me fate had something quite different in store. It all began with a note to me from the Marine Superintendent Bombay stamped: Urgent! It read: 'Kindly call at this office and see me this afternoon'. It was not unexpected, but not particularly welcome either, with its prospect of heading East for a few years. I had already left the *Gurna* on arrival in Bombay, moving to the hospital ship *Vasna* for transit purposes. From there I duly reported at the office of the 'Super' to learn my fate.

Chapter Three

From Red Ensign to Blue

Listening intently to what the Marine Superintendent was saying I soon realised that he was actually offering me the chance to serve as acting Third Officer on the Admiralty Salvage Vessel *Salviola*. She was bound for the Persian Gulf to remove wartime wrecks which were causing obstructions in politically sensitive locations. I would have to volunteer, as it meant serving outside the BI (British India) fleet. No, I didn't need to be given time to think it over, I knew that it was a rare opportunity to swap the Red Ensign for the Blue, and the mercantile routine for the exciting and unpredictable world of marine salvage.

I immediately signed off *Vasna* and onto *Salviola's* articles the next day, 11th April 1946, officially transferring my loyalties from the Captain of the *Vasna* to Captain Ritty of the *Salviola*. Life would never be quite the same again, as I soon found that this was not just another ship, but I had taken my place in the salvage team and, from then on, was to become more involved in the mystique of marine salvage than I had ever imagined possible.

On climbing aboard the *Salviola* as she lay at anchor in Bombay harbour, I found her to be a somewhat overgrown ocean-going tug. She was, however, carrying everything from de-compression chambers and machine workshops below decks to heavy lifting gear and fire fighting foam guns above. She was also bristling from stem to stern with a seemingly endless array of salvage equipment.

ASV Salviola

Alongside the *Salviola* lay a strange looking vessel which I later discovered to be a Royal Navy lifting craft. It was rather like a large sardine tin with goal post masts. It had accommodation for a crew, a boiler room (which provided power for heavy lifting winches and windlass) and the all important ability to flood and pump out the main compartments (which gave huge buoyancy for major lifts, submarine style). The lifting craft (LC) were, however, 'dumb barges' having no means of self-propulsion. Hence, our LC needed to hang on to *Salviola* ready to be towed across the Indian Ocean to Muscat. This was to be the scene of my first operation. The Norwegian freighter the *SS Dah-Pu* had been torpedoed while discharging cargo at anchor in the centre of the harbour. My overall impression as I tried to take in the full potential of my new home, was one of power, capability and independence.

Weighing in at 1100 tons gross and 200 feet in length, it was certainly the smallest ship I had served on. But as I surveyed the 22 inch (girth) Manila rope 'spring' which took the shock from the towing hawser, I was impressed. There was no time for any training, so it would be another case of picking it up as I went along, but then why change the habits of a lifetime?

Getting to know the rest of the team proved more complicated, as both the First Officer and No. 2 Diver were considered to be unfit for the gruelling conditions of the Gulf and were ordered home on medical grounds. This decision turned out to be fully justified by our later experience.

Another delay was caused by our Chief Engineer dropping heavily into the shore boat and breaking a bone in his foot. But finally, with added plaster, we were finally ready to sail on 1st May – exactly a year since my first ship *Neuralia* herself became a wartime casualty off the Italian coast. What a change of scene and how appropriate that I would now have the chance to take part in clearing up the mess we'd helped to make.

Lifting craft on short tow.

As we were one watch-keeper short, the Skipper took the 12-4 watch, the Second Mate the 4-8 and I stood my normal 8-12. Getting under way meant not only weighing the anchor but also paying out almost 1000 feet of wire towing cable from the stern (as thick as your wrist) before setting course. Although the traditional stations for us all leaving port would have sited me on the bridge, the First Mate on the fo'c'sle to deal with the anchor, and the second mate aft, as we were one short I was sent aft and found myself amidst the hectic activity of letting go the LC, passing it aft and paying out the towing wire without fouling the propeller. Luckily the crew were well trained in the task and I was only needed to pass on orders from the bridge without really knowing the routine to carry them out.

We eventually settled down to a towing speed of between four and five knots, and as the lifting craft was being towed unmanned and unlit, we needed to send radio warnings to all ships giving passage details so that, hopefully, no one would try to pass between us, with catastrophic results.

In fact, the voyage was largely uneventful, although due to the sky remaining overcast, we were forced to rely on dead reckoning to predict our landfall. So, when, on the last night before landfall, I suddenly got a brief clear glimpse of the moon on my watch I was tempted to chance a 'sight'. The ship's sextant obliged and it all looked good but it wasn't an obvious winner as, due to the proximity of the moon, large corrections had to be applied to the observation making the results generally unreliable. Undaunted, I settled down to the calculations but I found that it put us about forty miles south of our dead reckoning position. I quickly binned the workings and said nothing. The next morning, we made our landfall on the rocky coast and (surprise, surprise) we were forty miles south of Muscat. We therefore had to follow the coast for that distance before stopping engines two miles off the Muscat Cove in order to bring the lifting craft alongside. So I had missed my chance of glory there.

I had settled easily into the routine, things were pretty relaxed. No one needed a shirt except for meals. Our charismatic Skipper even favoured bare feet while at sea. My cabin was a few feet directly above the boiler tops and there was no cooling in our ventilation system, perhaps just as well, as we needed to acclimatize before Muscat.

Our salvage craft moored to the Dah-Pu.

As there would be no water available ashore, we had been running trials distilling salt water and thought we could get by. If not we would need to take it from visiting ships – assuming, of course, that there were any.

The Muscat that greeted us on 8ᵗʰ May as we moved in to anchor in the harbour was far removed from today's oil-rich capital city. Oil production only really started in 1964. At this time, Muscat lived under a very traditional Sultan whose palace (complete with Harem) overlooked the harbour. At each end of the water front stood a sixteenth-century fort. Both of these were in full use. Fort Jalali to the West was a prison, whose inmates were manacled by an iron bar between their ankles. Fort Merani on the Eastern flank was home to the Muscat Infantry who occasionally made their presence felt by firing 'Royal Salutes' from the ramparts using a spectacular battery of historic muzzle-loading cannons. In order to achieve the proper interval between shots, one man with a taper could be seen running frantically up and down the line to whichever crew was ready and had a hand raised. But the inevitable misfire occurred and we were always waiting for a ram-rod to come sailing out over the harbour. No such luck.

Our sister ship *Salvalour* had arrived ahead of us towing the second lifting craft. But she did not stay long after transferring her Second Mate to join us as our Chief Officer. This left us to carry out the operation using the two lifting craft housing the Fleet Salvage crew to deal with the badly damaged stern and provide wire lifting capability when the time came to move her into shallower water to make her seaworthy for her final voyage.

It had long been a tradition for visiting ships to paint their names on the rock faces of the cove, and we were greeted by 'SALVALOUR WOT NO VIOLA', in contemporary 'Chad' format, painted in huge white letters by the entrance to the cove. The other surprise was finding clay pots perched on every high point of the wreck as it sat on the bottom, in the middle of the cove, the water lapping the boat deck at high tide.

It was not long before the mystery was solved however, as the whine of high velocity bullets was followed by the spectacular shattering of a pot a few inches above our heads. Unbelievably, the Sultan, on his palace balcony, was pursuing his favourite hobby which was apparently rifle shooting, the clay pots being satisfying targets. That first night the salvage crew lost no time in removing this temptation under the cover of darkness. And shortly after, we inadvertently evened the score, by bringing down some of the Sultan's ceilings by slightly over-calculating the cutting charges we needed to sever the stern of the wreck.

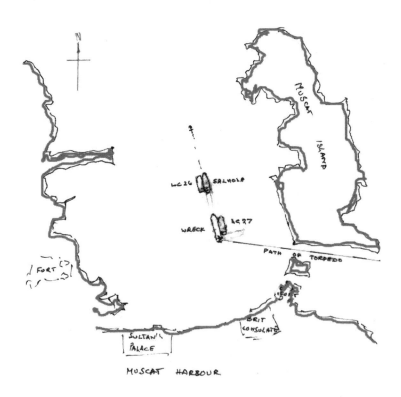

Sketch plan of Muscat harbour at the start of the operation.

The plan for the operation, formed after surveying the state of the hull, was to cut off the whole of the badly damaged stern (which had been almost, but not completely, severed by the explosion and now lay over on its port side), and float the remainder from bow to engine room. This would be achieved by extending the foredeck bulwarks up above the water level with a timber coffer-dam (water-tight wall) and sealing up all other openings below water level.

So we moored *Salviola* stern to the bow of the wreck with a lifting craft on either side of the damaged stern. Settling down to work through the long summer, we broke off only during the hottest part of the day (between 10am and 3.30pm).

The Dah-Pu and LCs against a back drop of the prison and Consulate.

After taking the plunge, our divers soon abandoned the traditional suits, unbearable in these temperatures, and resorted to skin diving but without the modern aqualung. So they started exploring the darkness of No. 1 hold clad only in shorts and using masks improvised from scrap service gas respirators connected to an air line and secured around the waist. But gasps greeted them when they first surfaced as they emerged covered head to foot with thick black bands – zebra fashion. During the four years that the wreck had been lying there, the cargo of bitumastic compound had escaped from the corroded barrels and was slowly making its way to the surface like a tropical forest. It was through this 'forest' that our unsuspecting divers swam with such dramatic results. The clean up that followed required their heads to be shaved.

Perhaps surprisingly we never stopped to consider why this unexciting cargo ship had been singled out for what must have been quite a hazardous operation for the submarine to undertake, requiring it to risk being beached in the shallow water in order to get into position to fire the torpedo through a gap in the chain of rocks which could be waded across at low tide. Certainly it was only years after that I discovered the *Dah-Pu* was listed under 'British naval vessels lost at sea', described as a 'Special Service Vessel', so maybe there was more to this sinking than we realized at the time.

The hot and sticky conditions in which we worked could only be relieved by diving over the side at frequent intervals. This also dealt with the thick coatings of sawdust which covered our bodies as we slaved over the circular saw, converting the roughly hewn timber 'jungle' sleepers we'd acquired, (as the only readily available timber we could get) into coffer-dam planks. Each sleeper would provide three planks.

It is not easy to describe the working conditions at this time except perhaps to recall that the most encouragement you could expect from your work mates was: 'You're not strong, you just smell strong!' I also discovered that if I kept my rubber boots full of sea-water when I returned from a dip, to resume cutting steel with an oxy-acetylene torch in the workshop, I avoided burns to my feet from molten metal dropping inside my sea boots, as it then merely raised plumes of steam. I soon became familiar with the intricacies of cutting threads on bolts, making patches and changing blades on the circular saw, buckled by the jungle sleepers as they twisted on their way across the saw bench. Gradually we were able to find and seal up the potential leaks in the bow section, in shade temperatures up to 120°F with percentage humidity in the high 90s. The most common problem seemed to be that of passing out from heat exhaustion and being brought round sharply by the searing heat of the steel deck penetrating your bare back.

The occasional need to make the trip along the coast in our general service boat to the Port of Mutrah provided a welcome break from the working routine. It was here that an American missionary had set up the *Knox Memorial Hospital* for the local people. It was the nearest medical assistance available to us, and consequently, I had to ferry a steady flow of crew members back and forth. But our involvement with the hospital soon included supplying it with empty bottles (beer bottles mainly) for medicinal re-use.

The Sultan pays a visit.

On one such delivery trip I saw a fascinating glimpse of life aboard the dhows. The dhows that called at Mutrah, sailed down to Zanzibar and across to Bombay, were large ornate craft. They had carved stern galleries, were beautifully maintained, 'varnished' with fish oils and rightly were a source of great pride to their skippers. But without engines, they were always glad to accept a tow from my work boat to get them out of the harbour to pick up the winds offshore.

On this occasion two rival owner/skippers were going ashore from their splendid vessels which were anchored off. Each launched a sleek long boat, no less decorated than their parent craft. Into these tumbled their dark-skinned brawny crews.

Last came the skippers who held the rudder heads to steer. The boats were pushed off and the oars duly rigged. The oars were not of the European pattern with their long curved blades. They had straight poles carrying square panels cornerwise at their ends and were decorated with ornate patterns.

The oars were held rigid, in a uniform and horizontal position while a rhythmic drum based chant started up, sung lustily by all hands. A long verse was followed by a short sharp dip of the oars with a strong pull, and a rapid return to the horizontal ready for the next verse. The chanting 'rest' period far exceeded the 'pull' phase, in contrast to our Western long steady sweeping action. So unless you were watching carefully, the 'pull' could easily be missed altogether and the oarsmen appeared just to be sitting motionless with their oars horizontal as the boats shot steadily across the water.

A dhow from my sketch book.

Sketch detail of boat oar.

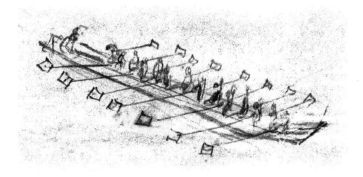

Dhow skipper going ashore from my sketch-book.

On approaching the shore, the pace quickened to a pull about every five seconds with everyone singing like mad to get through the verse in time, as the noise grew to a crescendo. Then on a signal from the silent skipper, the oars were shipped and brought inboard whilst the singing still continued, As the boats glided up to the quay, the now furious tempo of the chant was picked up by the rhythmic stamping of twenty pairs of feet, and accompanying hand claps. The singing finally stopped as the bowmen deftly brought the boats to rest alongside the quay.

It was quite a ceremonial ritual but nevertheless thoroughly enjoyed by all involved, and much more fun than my way of running the 'Old Man' ashore from the *Salviola*. I had never seen anything like this before and I felt privileged to have been there. What's more I have never found anyone else since who has witnessed anything like it.

Not all my boating escapades went smoothly however. One, in particular, put the boat out of action for a week, while our engineers made another prop shaft and rudder mountings in the machine shop. I had been asked to collect the Skipper and the Salvage Officer, a Lieutenant Commander RNVR, from a meeting at the Consulate ashore. I found them, looking unusually smart in their 'whites' standing on the stone waterfront above some submerged rocks. The rocks were revealed by the trough of each wave of the heavy swell that was running at the time.

I stood off and told them it wasn't possible to reach them in those conditions. But brushing aside my protests, the Skipper continued to order me in, until finally, in sheer desperation, I resolved that I would show him just how impossible it was by wrecking the boat.

I waited for the next big wave and angrily roared in alongside them on its crest, passing inches above the rocks. As one, they stepped smartly on board and, as I struggled to get us away, I found to my surprise that we were swept off again by the same retreating wave. We didn't get off scot-free though as the heavy vibration the boat now felt, plus a wonky rudder, confirmed we had caught the rocks a glancing blow as we left.

As I contemplated whether this was going to be enough to prove my point to the Skipper, the Salvage Officer leant over and quietly muttered into my ear:

"I think that was the finest feat of seamanship I have ever seen" Realizing that this was what it must have appeared to be – rather than the desperate act of defiance it really was – my frustration melted away. Although I still thought it had been a damned fool thing to have done, and consequently un-seamanlike,

I glowed with the compliment and decided that I'd better leave it at that as I headed off to make my peace with the engineers and persuade them to do the straightening out after this 'unfortunate accident'.

Living conditions on board only became a talking point when yet another of our wire framed camp beds ripped from end to end having rotted through continual saturation in sweat and deposited the body on the deck as he slept. Another blow was the loss of a batch of our precious gramophone records, which had been left standing in a cardboard box on the 'monkey island' (above the wheelhouse) and had been 'welded' into a solid mass by the sun, rather like a flat tyre. So when the opportunity came for us all to get away from it all for a spell and go ashore to play volleyball against the hospital team we jumped at it. We somehow scraped together a team in an assortment of kit. The First Mate, who was of fairly heavy build, couldn't find anything suitable to wear on his feet. After desperately scouring the ship, at the last minute, he triumphantly emerged with a pair of canvas, rope-soled shoes that fitted. He had found them at the bottom of a diving gear locker.

We were all surprised at his lacklustre performance, however. But we were more concerned when we found him sweating profusely and complaining that he felt about ninety. He was hardly able to drag himself around the court. It was only when stripping off for a shower, back on board, that he discovered to his infinite relief (and our great amusement) that his canvas shoes were actually divers' wading sandals which were 'ballasted' inside with thick lead insoles to keep them firmly on the bottom. Our team never looked back after that.

We were producing a steady stream of casualties at this time including one of our engine room artificers who had 108 boils on his body, none of which were healing after lancing, and even an RAF parachute drop of the new antibiotic Penicillin failed to shift them. One of our own native crew died after a bout of enteric fever even though he had returned from the hospital cured of the fever. He had lost so much weight that his friends all told him he looked like death, and he was so disturbed by this that within two days he had died. We made him a coffin and buried him in a graveyard outside the city, but by the next day he had been dug up again apparently to salvage the wood from the coffin.

Our contact with life ashore was definitely very limited, but we were aware that if you moved about after dark you had to carry a lantern, as there was a curfew to protect the locals from the attentions of marauding tribesmen. Anyone without a lantern was likely therefore to be shot at, and we certainly took this seriously. I therefore ensured that when I had to put our sick berth attendant ashore to go the hospital in Mutrah one night, he had a hurricane lamp with him in the boat. Unfortunately the tide was out and I could not land him on the quay, neither did I want to get beached on a falling tide. So tying a line onto a moored craft I paid this out astern telling him to take soundings over the bow with the boat hook and let me know when there was about two feet of water. I would then make the line fast, stopping us from getting washed ashore, we would light the lamp and over he'd go and wade ashore. At least that was the plan. As luck would have it he was sounding over the port bow but jumped from the starboard bow and disappeared completely plus lamp. He must have found a table of rock which was only on the port side, and needless to say he was only interested in getting to dry land after that with or without a lamp and fortunately for us all he made it to the hospital.

I was given an opportunity to get to know the hospital a bit better when I needed treatment for a poisoned leg, which seemed to be aggravated by the salt water. Surgery was prescribed and so I moved in to a private room and surveyed my new surroundings. When the locals had to be admitted they moved in with their families who looked after them and guarded them through the nights by sleeping on the flat roof with their weapons.

There were no nurses, and so I was put under the care of a young boy about 10-years old whose job it was buy food from the market and cook it for me, a system which I have to say worked surprisingly well. From my window I was able to watch the stately progress of the camel caravans coming in from the desert, and idly passed the time by counting them as they went past. I was amazed to find as many as 200 in one continuous line nose to tail.

My other form of entertainment was provided by the local school master and his 'sixth form' English class. Being the only European in the district I was apparently the ideal, albeit only, source of English conversation available to them. Therefore frequent unannounced visits to my bedside were made during the ten days of my incarceration. The conversations seemed to always take the same turn however and end up debating the reasons why 'The West' felt that they had a superior lifestyle to that of the Bedouin Arab. The arguments followed the line that when you reduced all human experience down to basic feelings of comfort, happiness, and health, how could anyone increase their perception of comfort and happiness by amassing a lot of wealth and expensive equipment? You could be comfortable or even more comfortable, but you couldn't go on being more and more comfortable in proportion to your wealth. Therefore was there any point in constantly striving to 'better oneself' and to look down on those who had very little.

By the end of my stay I was almost ready to agree with them and give up my ambitions to become stinking rich, and head for the dunes. I have to confess however that in some strange way it seems to have permanently changed my attitude to what I can only describe as the need to concentrate purely on making money.

How much things have been changed by the development of the oil production and the consequent transfer of wealth from the west. It would be interesting to test some of these theories on the Arabs of today.

Chapter Four

The Raising of the SS Dah-Pu

Coffer-dam intact and LCs preparing to lift.

Once back on board I found that the work on the coffer-dam, built around the fore-deck, was almost complete. And as we approached the prospect of actually moving the wreck further inshore, the work took on a new urgency. The plan was to pump out enough to get her afloat and then use the tide to get her as far inshore as we could. This would put a lot of the hull above the water at low tide enabling us to improve her floatability and make her seaworthy for the final voyage to deep water offshore.

By this time all the wreckage from the after end had been separately removed by the lifting craft, towed to sea and dumped. The stern section had been beached in the next bay, where we had also placed the funnel that had been cut off to save weight. By constantly running pump tests we were able to trace and deal with most of the leaks and assess the feasibility of the operation. By using our own engine room pumping capacity, plus that of portable pumps located on the wreck, we could achieve a total capacity of 2,200 tons per hour. This was enough to float her in 35 minutes. The damaged end would also need to be lifted by the LCs when the engine room was being pumped out so that it floated high enough to move inshore. At this point we were by no means sure what would happen when we tried to float her. Would the hull take the strain of a further beaching? Would she float on an even keel? Would the bulkheads hold against the unusual pressures?

At last, the day of the first move came, after making one or two false starts and dealing with further leaks, pumping was started in earnest and the LCs were hove down as they took the weight of the after end. It was 12th September, four months since our arrival. A pattern of mooring lines had been laid out to points on the shore. This effectively closed the port. Then as she began to break free from the bottom, the rising tide allowed the mooring lines to ease her inshore. It was quite a moment when we first noticed the signs of her rolling in the swell, and the first move allowed her to travel over 300 feet inshore. This was then followed shortly after by a further 200 feet into 20 feet of water at low tide, once the pumps had been re-rigged to adjust pumping heights. From here we carried out the final preparations to take her out.

The foredeck revealed for the first time.

In order to make her independent of wire lifts, we would have to redistribute weight and bring in ballast. So, we were glad to have rock ballast delivered by prisoner labour and loaded into No. 1 hold. It was, however, during this operation that we were given another glimpse of the reality of life ashore, making a deep impression on us at the time. During the ballasting operation the prisoners were freed from their ankle manacles so that they could move freely about the craft, manhandling the stone from the barge to the wreck's hold.

The unusual temptations that this temporary freedom presented were too much for one man, who was caught stealing a length of rope. As the penalty for theft ashore was the loss of a hand, we were reluctant to hand him over to the authorities and instead decided to leave their foreman to deal with him as he thought fit. After a brief discussion with the rest of the gang, he asked for a piece of tarred marlin (type of cordage) and made a sort of 'cat of nine tails' which they then used to give the offender ten lashings before resuming work. His shame turned into gratitude and we had no further trouble.

With the combination of the stone ballast, the coal moved forward from the bunkers, the removal of all excess weight from the after end, and the unlikely practice of pumping water back in to the forepeak tank we judged that we had achieved a more even trim at last.

Dah-Pu beached inshore towers over us.

Unfortunately, working on board at this time was none too pleasant, as the many species of marine life that had found the sunken hull to be their ideal home for the past few years were now in the early stages of decomposition after being unceremoniously brought out of the water. The result was a powerful stench which seemed to get progressively worse. It was poor reward for all the endless hours of fascination provided for us by these creatures who had just made an unfortunate choice of home.

Clearing the harbour.

By this time Salviola's bottom also needed the attention of our divers to remove the heavy growth of weed and barnacles not to mention a few quite large bushes which had taken root while we had been static. Nothing would be allowed to impede our progress to Bombay and then Colombo once we had finished in Muscat.

On 7th October the tides and conditions looked to be right, and we commenced the final stage of the operation. After pumping her 'dry' she was floating upright and by running the pumps at intervals through the night we kept her stable. At dawn we took off all superfluous gear and pumps leaving only two of the 6" motor pumps set up on the foredeck where they could be reached for rapid removal. Their task would be to maintain the levels in the engine room.

With some excitement we let go our stern moorings, started heaving in our anchor and paying out the towing hawser and bridle. By 8am our towing hawser was clear and we gave three blasts on our siren. This was the signal for the LCs to slip the wreck's moorings and let us go. We were on our way and the *Dah-Pu* was starting to follow us!

Pumping all the way!

She emerged, nose in the air, well down by the stern but with all the dignity of an aristocrat walking to the gallows; a long 'paying off pennant' flew from her foremast respecting Naval tradition for a ship on her last voyage; and a small salvage crew of engineers remained on board to keep those vital pumps running throughout the passage.

It was with considerable relief we reached the position we'd selected for the scuttling without incident and found the depth of water we needed.

On the way and going well.

Moving in for the kill.

Letting go the tow, we manoeuvred alongside her and recovered the last pumps and remaining salvage gear using our derricks. This was an anxious 15 minute operation during which she was already starting to settle.

Easy does it!

Once all the salvage gear had been removed, we stood off and plotted our position for the records while the engineers opened the sluice valves which we had fitted in the after engine room bulkhead to serve as scuttling ports.

One of the launches, that had escorted her all the way from the harbour, moved in to pick up the salvage crew. We could then do no more than wait patiently at a respectful distance. At first she seemed to be fighting her fate, but then settled more positively by the stern, and as the water began pouring in through the side doors, there was a dull rumbling roar as a bulkhead went and then up came the bow with the stem high above water, whilst at the same time the after end was submerging amidst a flurry of foam.

Pausing for a moment, she gave a slight shudder, and finally slid gracefully beneath the surface, throwing up a tall plume of spray as she did so. The *Dah-Pu* had died as only a ship can die, with majestic grace and at the end with awe-inspiring speed. All that remained was a patch of turbulence on the surface; we had achieved our goal and now had merely to pick up the bits we'd set aside in the next bay and we would be able to move out.

Spirits were high as we returned to anchor in the harbour and we lost no time in dispatching a diving party to the next bay to locate and prepare the bits of wreckage – not of course forgetting the funnel (still intact). All of this would need to be taken out to deep water and dumped.

Here goes . . .

To our surprise the divers returned looking rather subdued. They were, in fact, slightly embarrassed. Pressing them for an explanation, it gradually emerged that although they knew exactly where they had put the funnel, it was no longer there. What's more they hadn't been able to find it during a wider sweep. It was not until the next day that they discovered that it had been rolled by the undertow for a surprising distance.

Muscat Harbour cleared . . . job done.

Things then moved rapidly. We lashed the funnel alongside us, and piled it high with the other bits of wreckage, before steaming out to deep water where we cut the lashings. Perhaps it wasn't so surprising that we were known in the fleet as 'Captain Ritty's Travelling Circus'.

Chapter Five
Life After Muscat

Our somewhat lingering departure from Muscat was due more to the need to tow both lifting craft back to Bombay in succession than any reluctance on our part to say goodbye. But we did manage a full dress farewell dinner for all our shore based friends at a long table set up under an awning on the flag-decorated lifting craft. A few whoops on our siren as we drew out of the harbour next morning told the world that we really were off this time.

Our tow struggling.

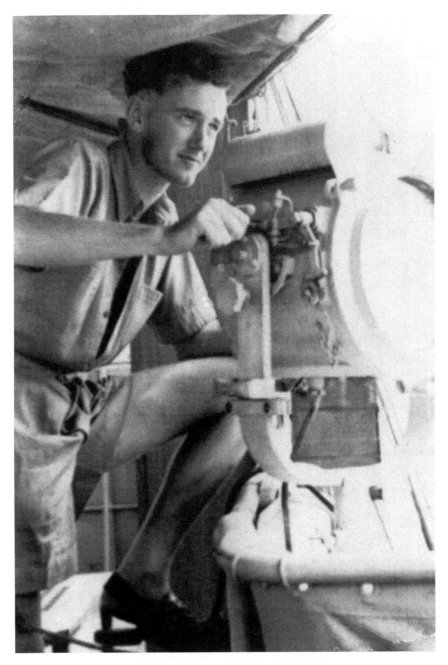

The author manning the signal / search-light.

Then, as if to remind us that we were still basically seamen, and had not reverted to landlubbers, we were treated to a cyclonic storm in mid-ocean with predicted hurricane force winds which effectively killed our towing speed from our usual four knots so that during some four-hour watches we only made about three miles. We certainly couldn't risk snapping the towing line as we didn't have the fuel to go and look for our tow in those conditions – even supposing that we would have been able to see anything beyond the confines of the ship. Everyone lost interest in eating, and we were all reduced to munching cream crackers with marmalade for a couple of days – purely from choice as we explained to each other.

Life on board as we weathered the storm meant coping with the violently pitching vessel as it struggled to haul the tow up one wave whilst plunging down another some distance ahead, only to be held back by the tow, which had the alarming effect of making parts of the ship rise and fall faster than by gravity.

Climbing the bridge ladder meant hanging on in such a way that you kept your feet clamped onto the treads in order to keep some sort of control on your movements. Even more exciting were the visits by the officer of the watch to inspect the condition of the huge rope 'spring' which was sawing back and forth over the towing bars. Without these bars which arched over the after deck, the crew were in danger of being swept overboard as the tow veered from side to side.

The sawing motion would gradually wear through the strands of the rope causing it ultimately to part, with disastrous consequences had it not been for the way we had 'parcelled' the rope with heavy leather and rope yarn all covered with thick layers of tallow continually applied by a deck hand stationed underneath.

My most vivid memories of this time were going down from the comparative sanity of the bridge in the pitch darkness at the end of a night watch to this violently leaping and plunging deck. By then the tallow dripping from the towing spring ensured that the steel deck plating was covered with a thick slippery coating thus producing a rare combination of skating rink and big dipper. Any signs of wear were hopefully revealed by your torch as you craned your neck up whilst hanging on desperately with your other hand. One minute buried in the boiling sea, the next yanked high in the air.

It was with considerable relief therefore that we left the second LC at Bombay, and sailed on unhampered to Colombo, where we were told our weariness would be acknowledged with a little local leave up in the hills at the Naval Rest Centre.

On our return from Diyatalawa, where we had been enjoying English type weather for a few days, we descended to hot and steamy Colombo to find that *Salviola* had also been receiving some rejuvenation treatment. Not withstanding our divers' furious efforts to scrape the trees and bushes off her bottom before we left Muscat, we found her hiding in a giant dry dock with only her masts showing above the parapet. Unlike most of the salvage fleet which was now being laid up we were getting a much needed servicing and the addition of generators which would permit us to shut down the main engines, and carry on operating. This was in preparation for our next challenge which we were told was the removal of the Shah's Steam Yacht *Ivy* which had sunk at a jetty in the Persian Navy's base at Khorramshar, between Abadan and Basra.

* * *

Duly refreshed and re-equipped, we sailed for Bombay in January 1947 to pick up a re-fitted LC before heading for the Persian Gulf with an extra stop at Bahrain. Our task was to float a beached and abandoned River Gunboat *HMS Seamew* by hauling her into deeper water using wire tackles secured to a manual 'windlass' on an abandoned barge which happened to be suitably located.

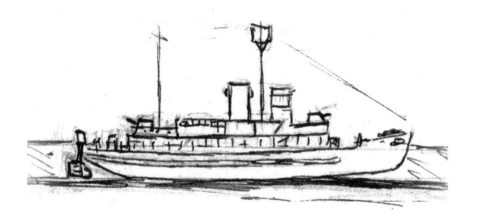

Sketch of Seamew grounded.

I hadn't met one of these vessels before, but could well imagine her flying the flag in a tricky Colonial situation as she steamed boldly up some muddy river to rescue Carruthers while the drums sounded out through the jungle around her. She was flat-bottomed with a very shallow draft and had propellers in tubes but otherwise was a fully functioning miniature warship.

Deeper Water

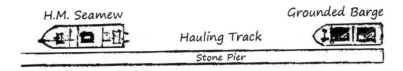

The scene for the proposed move.

Our orders were to float her and make her ready to be towed to Karachi by a Naval tug. Although we stopped her leaks and moved her two hundred feet in barely enough water for her six foot draft, this revealed that her flat bottom was paper thin in places. After thorough examination, we decided that her hull was in such poor condition we had no option but to report that she was not seaworthy and would therefore be left where she was for dismantling.

In order to reach this conclusion we had, of course, sent a working party to bivouac on board the *Seamew* as she lay alongside a shallow water quay in Khan Kalijah. *Salviola* had to remain in a safe deeper water anchorage some distance off in Sitrah Bay. This meant a seven mile run in the service launch and negotiating narrow channels between sandbanks and coral reefs to reach the casualty.

Going aboard the *Seamew* with food to cook, a small generator, tools and equipment, we were met by two Arab watchmen whose job it was to look after her. They introduced themselves as Sahif and Abdullah. I noticed that Sahif passed his time basket-making from local grasses. I decided he should be commissioned to make me a straw hat to work in. This seemed to be a whole new experience to him, but after a few false starts and a lot of sketches, my hat emerged. It fitted and was a glorious testimony to his skill.

Straw hat in use.

The hat survived to look after me for the whole of the rest of my salvage career.

Although the ship had been derelict for many years, our one chance of achieving hot food was to get the galley stove (situated in its deck house) working. Darkness had fallen, so we lit improvised oil lamps (made from beer cans filled with paraffin into which wicks were pushed) as our little generator could only manage to light up the main saloon. We soon realized that the thick black smoke which filled the galley, making it impossible to see how our bacon and eggs were doing, could not have been caused by the lamps. The stove flue must have been blocked. Remembering that I had seen a skylight in the roof of the deckhouse right above the stove, I leapt up to lever it open. Unfortunately, it resisted and my more vigorous attempts resulted in the whole skylight structure coming off the deck in my hands, amidst an unseen shower of rust and flakes.

It was only when we proudly carried the delicious smelling fry-up to the brightly-lit saloon to place before our shipmates that we found to our dismay the whites of the eggs were all grey and studded with large pieces of rust. Luckily the party's uncharacteristic hesitation in the presence of food was soon overcome when they were told we'd used up all the supplies we'd brought (helped no doubt by a fortuitous issue of 'Navy Neaters' rum ration).

Our attempts to sleep in one of the cabins which had berths but no mattresses led to us being sliced up by the diamond wire mesh of the bed frames. At about two o'clock we were all awake and I suddenly remembered the Chief Steward pressing a thermos flask into my grasp as we left the ship. The thought of that hot coffee got everyone struggling up again and once I'd rummaged around in the dark and found the flask I quickly poured out some cups and the gang took greedy gulps only to spit it straight out again. It turned out to be thick tomato soup, perfectly wholesome but definitely not the coffee everyone was anticipating. What with that and the purgatorial bunks, we abandoned all pretence of sleep and as dawn broke I set off back wrapped in a blanket against the bitter cold. By the time I reached the ship I was soaked by the icy spray, and lost no time getting under the hot shower.

Possibly this rich experience made such an impression on me at the time that when writing home some time later I decided to give the whole episode a more poetic if not romantic slant. I wrote:

"I'm now going to take you back (for no reason at all) to that dreamy shore of Bahrain. On the end of a concrete pier, bleached and baked by an unrelenting sun, a motley gang of Arab coolies sweat and toil at wires and blocks, pumps and hoses, as a forty ton purchase is dragged, pushed and wrenched out from the muddy foreshore onto a derelict wreck of a barge, thence to a waiting dhow."

Lament for the Seamew

Higher and higher in the heavens the sun rises,
ounce by ounce human energy is sapped and
slower and more sluggish become the efforts of that hapless band.
Others there are, still of that band, who labour yet upon the ship
– the ship that lived and died –
died not a heroine's death,
but crept meekly to a foreign shore to lay her weary bones –
and move no more.

Too late she heard the call! The call to sea and action – that she loved:
too late the noise of feet upon her decks:
too late the merry voice within her sounds:
the tempting galley smells abound –
the ship is dead!
There on the pier what see we now? – the Arab half castes toil no more
but slink exhausted to the shade pausing only to wrap a fragment of filthy
rag – now soaked with sweat – about their heaving bodies.
And so 'tis now the order clear: Retire!
Take back these hopes of rousing an old spirit,
shaking an old frame,
and leading her on to further glory.
– For here's no ship. Here lies a hulk. The Seamew is no more.

* * *

It was whilst on this operation that my lifelong love of boat handling nearly proved my undoing. I endeavoured to get my hands on the ship's twenty-eight foot General Service Launch at every opportunity as I have previously explained. It was built with twin skin mahogany planking to classic sea boat design and fitted with a large powerful diesel engine.

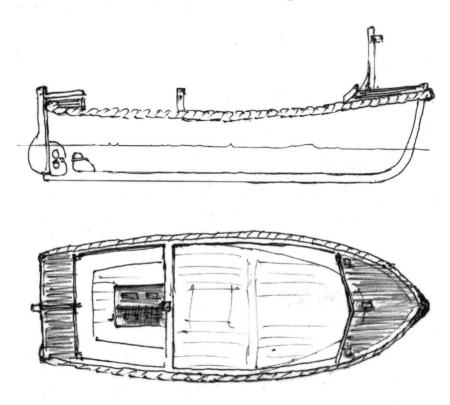

28' General Service Launch.

To me, it was happiness afloat and capable of making coastal passages. Perhaps it was not surprising, therefore, that I found myself always in demand to run people ashore at all hours of day and night without waiting for any other boat's crew, and with scant regard for consequences.

On one occasion, I was returning alone late one night from the jetty at Bahrain, looking for the entrance to the channel with my 'Aldis' signal lamp used as a search light when, without warning, the engine spluttered and became silent. All my attempts to re-start it failed as, fatefully, our last supply of fuel was later found to have been contaminated. Taking a quick look around with my 'Aldis' lamp as I was carried out to sea by the tide, my second sweep picked out a small mooring buoy which by lucky chance, I was rapidly approaching on the starboard bow.

To my great relief, my rather desperate efforts using the boat hook as an oar brought the buoy within my reach, a mighty effort saw me securely moored and my steady progress out to sea halted. I was then able to contemplate my chances of rescue more calmly. Clearly, the Aldis lamp held the key to rescue but by whom? The distant lights of *Salviola* were visible as she lay at anchor, but I knew no watch was being kept and in any event she had no other boat easily available.

Then my hopes were raised as I spotted a new arrival, a British warship was now moored a little further off and they would certainly have a watch system. Here was my chance. Despite diligent efforts to master the Morse code, most Merchant seamen were no match for the speed of the Navy's professional signalmen. In the days of the Convoys when we often found ourselves replying to the bewildering speed of a Naval vessel's signal lamp, we would take refuge in the practice of sending the Morse letter 'W' which, according to the Convoy signal book, had the meaning: 'You should focus your lamp better, I am unable to read your signal'. Eventually the exasperated Naval signalman would slow right down to dictation speed and we stood a chance to work out the message.

This was undoubtedly an emergency and I had to take them on, so training my 'Aldis' on the warship I called them up. To my great relief the flash of a signal lamp appeared out of the darkness, they replied almost immediately. I cryptically explained who I was, what had happened and asked for assistance. Whether they were able to read it all I never knew but thankfully they decided to come and investigate.

When their well-manned boat finally came alongside, my main problem seemed to be convincing them that this was all in my regular line of duty. I had no other crew, my engine had failed, I had picked up the buoy by chance; and I merely sought the means to complete my journey. I don't think they ever quite believed me but they towed me straight back to *Salviola* (to the surprise of my shipmates), and agreed to rendezvous with, and bring back, our shore party, and settle for our warm thanks. God bless the Navy!

Chapter Six

We Meet the *Ivy*

Having wound our way up the Shatt El Arab river, and delivered the LC to an oil jetty in Abadan we left her there to deal with a sunken gunboat to be operated by a Naval Salvage team while we pressed on up the river to the Hafar Channel where the Royal Persian Navy had its base at Khorramshar. There we found the Steam Yacht *Ivy* lying at one of the jetties, listing over and submerged up to her boat deck. Once the pride of a Sheikh and more recently the Shah, unfortunately she had been allowed to sink, apparently through failure to pump the bilges. Obviously some misunderstanding must have occurred, but Britain's obligation to clear her away from this jetty was accepted.

THE IVY IN HER PRIME.

My sketch on arrival showing how I thought she would have looked afloat.

As it was then in January 1947 Persia/Iran presented a strange mixture of contrasts especially as seen from the Persian Naval Base; ornate minarets and mud huts; glossy American cars and ox carts; highly polished jack boots and rags, a country about to change.

Losing no time to assess the 'casualty' we took a closer look at *Ivy*'s situation and made our first shock discovery – she was full of mud almost to water level. Perhaps not surprisingly bearing in mind her situation, she seemed to be intact and certainly undamaged. Almost entirely built of teak, above and below decks; she had square openings in the hull for portholes, looking like gun ports, and there was still a wealth of copper visible on deck such as ventilation cowls, clearly she had been kept effectively guarded within the base.

Alongside the Ivy.

The main priority was obviously to clear the mud out as far as possible, then attempt to seal up the entire hull and deck houses, and by pumping and hauling her more upright, get her floating sufficiently to tow her away to a final beaching berth further up the channel where she could be safely dismantled.

The temperature at this time of year, coupled with the type of diving activity we were undertaking, dictated that this work would be best carried out using traditional (Siebe Gorman) suits the design of which has changed little in the last fifty years. This gave me a wonderful opportunity to become familiar with the mysteries of this very fundamental manner of diving. Each diver had a 'linesman' whose job it was to dress and undress him, man his air line when submerged and communicate via a coded series of tugs on the line. The heavy rubberised fabric suit was in one piece, entered feet first through the helmet hole, and although the feet remained enclosed the hands were forced out through tight cuffs, helped by a lot of Vaseline. Once in the suit, heavily ballasted boots, weighing 17lbs each were laced on (to keep him the right way up), then a metal 'corselet' was inserted and bolted into the helmet hole providing the mounting for the helmet which then locked on with a quarter turn.

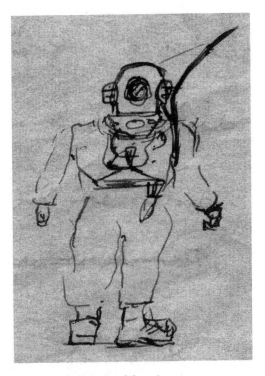

Sketch of diver's suit.

When ready the helmet would be finally sealed up by the fitting of the 'face glass', which also screwed on, enabling him to look out. Just for good measure, lead weights were attached on the back and chest totalling a further eighty pounds; normally these were added while he was standing on the ladder. A belt and diving knife went on round the waist to complete the kit. It was this knife that made me wonder if I had it in me to be this kind of diver.

Ivy's boat deck looking aft.

The reason for this was that our leading diver, who was now missing the best part of three fingers on his left hand, had had to use his rusty diving knife to cut them off when they became trapped by a wire under a wreck which was starting to roll onto him some years previously. I really didn't know if I would be able to do that when it came to the point, but luckily the test never came.

So for the time being I was happy to do the linesman bit, and with practice we got the dressing process down to about seven minutes, but nevertheless the demand for a last minute pee just before going down or indeed just after, met a less than enthusiastic reaction. Once the helmet was on, the air line from it was passed under the arm and tied to the side of the helmet thus ensuring that if the air line had to be used to haul him, the pull would be properly controlled. The buoyancy of the suit was controlled by the diver adjusting the spring loaded escape valve on his helmet. He had to avoid screwing it right up in a panic, as it then became impossible for him to release it again. The suit rapidly inflated to become rigid in the shape of a star fish and it was then quite impossible for him to bend his arm to reach it with his hand. This would be followed inevitably by a rapid uncontrolled ascent to the surface where he would be forced to remain floating until rescued, not only suffering the consequences of the uncontrolled ascent but also facing the prospect of suffering the further indignity of having to scrub out his suit to remove the consequences of the fright. This was not traditionally part of the linesman's duties.

But now, all efforts needed to be concentrated on methods for removing that mud which seemed to be solidly filling all parts of the hull. After various experiments we evolved a system which relied on the strum box of a six inch suction hose fitted by our engineers with a compressed air nozzle pointing up the pipe, fed by a separate air line. This would break up the mud released by a powerful hose allowing it to be sucked out and discharged by the salvage pumps. Getting the water / mud ratio right took a while, but once achieved our mud larking never looked back.

As we probed further and further into the interior, I was able to advance my plans which enabled us to design and make the appropriate panels and patches to seal her up.

Pumping mud . . .

We found that the smaller pumps were quite unable to cope with the mud and choked up at once but the big diesel and steam pumps of 6"and 10" diameter really delivered the goods. 'The Windy Lift' as it became known served us throughout the operation, and with the grill removed from the business end it would gobble up practically anything. From now on it was sheer slog as we ate our way slowly through the interior, compartment by compartment.

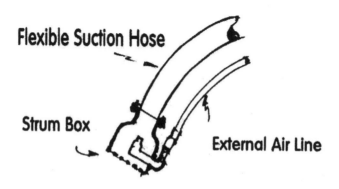

Detail of mud ejector.

We were able to break the monotony somewhat by running a ship's cinema, as we had been members of the RN Film Library for some time now, and consequently one of the first questions we would ask a visiting Naval vessel would be 'What films have you got?'

I had taken the projector under my care and protection and was therefore responsible for putting on the shows, furthermore I found that I was able to improve the rather dodgy sound reproduction by re-focusing the light beam onto the sound track. I felt confident therefore in setting up a huge screen on the jetty instead of the usual poky screen possible in our restricted accommodation, so we would be able to have our own open air cinema.

The test film I ran before every performance was a short cartoon of jungle animals singing 'Icky Ticky Tambo Za Za Rambo, Ba Ba Rosca Boom' as they swung from tree to tree, and this tested the equipment very nicely. To the local children from the base however, this became our signature tune and an appropriate greeting should they see one of us in the base. What was more surprising was the fact that families turned up in such numbers that there was often no room for our crew. But frequently this only lasted through the test film after which they would all get up and walk out, as the feature film rarely had the same universal appeal.

We had also made good connections with one or two of the Anglo Iranian Oil Co's engineers in Abadan and were able to visit them in their villas on the residential estates, courtesy of the free bus service from the base. Strangely these desert buses could always be identified by the fact that they always seemed to travel leaning heavily to one side as everyone sat on the shady side to keep cool.

As the mud content of the wreck gradually reduced, we were able to turn our attention to preparing for righting her which included rigging additional stays for the masts so that they were better able to take the pull of the wire purchases from the shore. We also tried to make it easier for her to break free by clearing the river bed mud from under her starboard bilge (the high side).

Our first attempts revealed the weaknesses but showed little success, and it was decided to sweep wires under her bow and bring in some 'camels' which were normally well-controlled buoyancy tanks which could be sunk, connected to wire strops under the hull and then blown with compressed air in a carefully controlled manner. Unfortunately these camels had no subdivision so that as soon as air was introduced they tended to stand on end with dire results; however we persevered and after learning many new circus tricks, including the art of standing on rapidly spinning semi-submerged tanks we did see signs of movement.

Ivy's bow with Persian Naval Fleet beyond.

Throughout the operation I should explain that we were of course maintained by an unfailing supply of beer from the Naafi at Basra, the main problem being that of delivery over land which was really too great to contemplate, especially getting it into the base. We therefore managed to evolve a cunning plan with the help of the Royal Naval patrol ship which passed regularly down the Shatt Al Arab river from Basra to the Gulf and open water.

A camel misbehaving.

Having loaded our Naafi order onto their quarterdeck they would slow down when still well upstream from Khorramshar and rendezvous with our service launch which would be waiting nearby to speed in alongside and do a rapid transfer.

We would then disappear into the reeds on the river bank and creep quietly round into Hafar Channel whilst the patrol vessel picked up speed and proceeded down river past the Persian Naval base with Hands lining the rails observing full ceremonial saluting procedure; this of course was being acknowledged by the base with their personnel drawn up on the parade ground.

By the time the base returned to normal we had everything stowed away, and were working normally. It was a system which served us well and one that we considered essential to our survival if somewhat unorthodox.

The stern comes afloat.

Our relationship with the Officers of the base had gradually improved to the point of us being entertained to receptions which involved toasting the Shah and our Monarchy with spirits of totally unrecognisable origin which registered the following morning however when we attempted to get our heads off our pillows.

For our part we had put out a fire in their base ahead of their fire brigade, and fielded numerous questions from those attempting to make their ex-Italian Gunboats work properly. One such problem which was relayed to us revealed a surprising lack of understanding, and involved the basic propulsion of the vessel. Apparently when they started the engines (we had in fact noticed the flames shooting out of the funnel), and then tried to turn the 'axle' (propeller shaft) the engines moved forward several inches on their mountings. We found on investigation that the essential 'thrust blocks' which transfer the thrust of the propellers to the hull of the ship had been completely removed, but luckily not dumped.

We also offered to correct the charts they would need in the Gulf as they were all found to be woefully out of date. We felt therefore we had built up some degree of mutual understanding, if not respect, and recognition of this was soon evidenced by an invitation to a party held on the departure of all the Officers' wives, who were accustomed to leave the base for the summer months and go to live up in the hills. To our surprise however as the dust cloud disappeared to the north another appeared to the south which proved to be a troupe of gipsy dancing girls who moved swiftly in, to fill the void, so to speak. The resultant party performance and its aftermath remain a somewhat blurred but happy memory, but one which made us feel that we had finally been accepted.

Ivy on her last voyage, not quite the ship she had been.

As the temperature rose, there was no slackening of effort although we were able to return to skin diving, though this did have its disadvantages as I found when surfacing in the river to be hit in the face by the bloated corpse of some animal drifting down stream. This coincided with an infection by ringworm which rapidly spread to cover most of my face. Our Skipper's remedy involved painting my face several times a day with double strength iodine until the skin literally burnt off, worms and all. During this period Frankenstein had my full sympathies and I was forced to stay out of sight or risk gasps of horror.

I can best describe the scene on the wreck in the words of a letter home at this time. 'This stricken ship once the pride of a fleet has now become a hive of activity. Gangs of dark skinned men heave on tackles and ropes, pulling great pumps into position on the sloping deck, perhaps the roar of a motor pump being tested, or the huge steam pumps shaking the very beams of the ship as they throw their muddy burden far out over the side. The whine of a circular saw fills the air, then nearer still, drowning the rhythmic chanting of the heaving crew, a pneumatic drill coughs and groans its way through a baulk of timber as the work goes doggedly on.

The survivors who finally made it (with author top left).

We lost a bit of impetus when some of the salvage crew reached the end of their contracts and opted to return to the UK but, with a few new faces, the Skipper and I kept going to see it through, and the slight pause gave us the chance to bring in yet more pumps.

Ivy sitting pretty at the end of it all.

We then entered a phase of frequent pumping tests, patching and repairing where leaks were spotted, until finally on 21st October, some ten months after our arrival and with an impressive 3,800 tons of water per hour being shifted we were able to discard the camels and float her free of Salviola. We disconnected all our own pumping connections and left the motor pumps holding their own.

Having started pumping at 4a.m. in order to make best use of the tide, within two hours we were able to leave her in the care of two of the Oil Co's tugs to make the passage upstream.

Once she had reached her allotted berth she was scuttled and settled down in good trim ready for stripping down and well clear of the operational Naval Base. It took no more than a few days for us to retrieve all our salvage gear with the aid of a floating crane, then pickup LC27 from Basra and make everything ready for the long slow tow home to Trincomalee calling at Bombay and Colombo before the last slog up the coast to Trinco.

Job done! Jetty back in use and we make ready to depart.

Footnote:

Although we never did mange to reveal the whole of *Ivy* when we floated her, many years later when in the Stores of the National Maritime Museum at Greenwich I stumbled across the shipyard half hull model.

I am very pleased to be able to include a picture of this model by their kind permission.

Ivy's Shipyard Model © NMM

Chapter Seven

Time to go Home

It was on the last leg of our slog back to Trincomalee dragging our unwilling LC behind us that tempers showed signs of fraying. The Skipper had not been keen to keep our tow all the way up the East coast of Ceylon from Colombo to Trincomalee as there was a known strong current of up to 4 knots at this time of year which would be against us. When towing this would leave us little scope for real progress over the ground. However, 'orders is orders', and we duly set off.

Our reluctant follower.

We rounded the south east corner of the island on my watch. My half-hourly bearings of the coast, when plotted on the chart came closer and closer together. We were running into treacle! Coupled with that, visibility reduced dramatically, and we were soon out of touch with our surroundings running on dead reckoning but without any reliable indication of the speed we were making good over the ground. After we had been groping our way up the coast on soundings for some time we turned inshore hoping to identify our location on the coast, but nerves failed when we could hear the surf on the beach but could still see nothing. Reporting our problem to the Fleet HQ we received a cheerful offer of assistance from HMS *Birmingham* who happened to be moored in Trinco harbour, she would take radio bearings of our signals and give us the details so that we could plot our position tied in with soundings. Wonderful! We carefully relayed all the details onto our chart and worked out ETAs and things and relaxed.

Quartermaster at the wheel.

Sparks (our radio operator) suddenly re-appeared on the bridge with another signal which he nervously put in front of the Skipper. From Lieut (Navigating Officer) *Birmingham* to Capt Ritty *Saviola* 'Regret to inform you all previous bearings subject to a repeater error of 15 degrees please apply correction to all bearings so far received'.

I thought the Old Man was going to explode, certainly the chart room was not the place to be at that time, and although the new information was quickly plotted and our position suitably revised, he refused to believe that it was any more reliable.

It was into this scenario that Sparks re-appeared bearing yet another signal from our mentor and guide, the contents of which produced an even more violent reaction: 'Would advise you that the southerly current on east coast of Ceylon is reduced to 1½ to 2 knots'. Grabbing the signal pad the Skipper savagely scribbled a reply:

"I can't send that Sir!" said Sparks.

"Yes you can, and will", Skipper barked. When I caught up with it I found it to be a respectful request that in view of his latest information, it was necessary to formally ask that the speed of Ceylon should now be reduced by 2 knots to allow us to catch up.

It was just our luck that as we were creeping into the Boom Defence base in Trinco by the early light of dawn, who should come steaming out in all her glory, with all hands lining the rails, but HMS *Birmingham*. The Skipper seemed to be preoccupied on the other wing of the bridge when their signal lamp started blinking. We needn't have worried however, the Navy's traditional good humour had prevailed, 'From Lieut N to Capt Ritty *"Congratulations on catching us up"*.

The time soon came to hand *Salviola* over to the Care and Maintenance Branch in her Boom Defence berth in Trincomalee, haul down our Blue Ensign, and bid both her and our old shipmates a fond farewell. Packing our kit involved a strange assortment of baggage, from canvas kit bag (made specially for me by one of our divers on his first night in port, despite my protests), to dubiously soldered tin trunks from the local bazaar, which in the event failed to justify their makers' claims.

But above all else I was to receive my most treasured possession to date – my reference from the Master of the *Salviola* which in future years would prove to me if proof were needed, that I really had done these extraordinary things.

Bo. No. 455.

British India Steam Navigation Co., Ltd.
(Incorporated in England)

XXX **A.S.V. SALVIOLA.** _____ Voy. No. **2** _____

_____ 20th. Dec. _____ 194**7**.

Mr. I.A. Milner.   TRINCOMALEE.

This Officer joined this Vessel while a Cadet, he is leaving
now 20-12-47, on the closing down of the Salvage Organisation.
A most experienced, capable and trustworthy Officer with a full
understanding of all the equipment and trades such as:- Burners,
Welders, Shipwrights and Divers used in Salvage work, having
practised all of them during his Services.

He has taken a very large part in the two major Salvage
Operations, each of nine months, in Muscat and Khorramsharh in
extremely hot weather. During these Operations he has supervised
most of the work, always being the Officer-in-charge of the
Casualty.

He has been Officer-in-charge of a Watch during 8,000 Deep
Sea Towing miles in all types of weather. This puts a lot of extra
responsibility on the Officer of the Watch.

He is a keen and careful Navigator fully capable of carrying
out any duty entrusted to him.

I wish him every Success and Prosperity for the Future.

Signed. ....

MASTER.

Two of us were to rejoin our Company in Bombay to find a passage home, whilst the rest of the crew were repatriating from Ceylon. The journey to Bombay by train would take the next three days and nights, using many different types of propulsion, not to mention the inevitable ferry.

The first leg of our journey, which took us across the island through the forests to the ferry point for the mainland, was rather overshadowed by the fact that the local boy who had been helping me on *Salviola*, was so desperate to come with us that he travelled for the first few miles clinging to the roof of our train, pleading through the window, before finally accepting the need to say goodbye.

This part of the journey was punctuated by stops at clearings in the forest which we discovered were to re-fuel our wood burning steam locomotive from the stacks of logs left there for that purpose.

Locomotives Indian style.

Once on the mainland, we settled into our coupé compartment with en suite shower and enjoyed the service provided by our smartly uniformed 'boy' who brought all our meals to us, and drinks (provided we were not passing through a State which had prohibition at the time).

Settling down for the night with a backdrop of romantically moonlit desert brought with it a rather shocking awakening next morning. We found ourselves peering at a sea of grinning faces framed in the window. We had pulled up at a wayside halt, complete with its inevitable band of urchins keen to take advantage of any passing trade. Luckily one of the many blinds soon dealt with this and we would know better next time. A change of trains at Madras, a stretch of the legs and we were on the last lap to Bombay where we finished the trip under overhead power lines. Thus we completed our progression through the development of motive power from jungle logs to coal, oil and finally electricity.

SS Pachumba

On arrival in Bombay I was sent to the *Gamaria* for a few days to await the *Pachumba* – a flush decked general cargo carrier whose black funnel with two white bands, announced to the world that she was a BI ship. The *Pachumba* represented my ticket home and so I gladly accepted reverting to Cadet again and believe it or not I was to be responsible for a strange collection of animals. These included two deer, one leopard cub, twelve monkeys, eleven horses and four pet dogs, not to mention a buffalo and calf to be dropped off at Karachi. It was not quite the farm I had on the *Gurna*, more a floating wild life park with racing overtones. They all arrived on the morning of the day we sailed leaving little time to get to know their funny little ways, not to mention their many and varied dietary preferences. Fortunately, we were given an aide memoire on a few sheets of paper plus the stores and straw bales to go with it.

Life on board would certainly not be dull, and quite a contrast with the two years' hard labour I had just completed, particularly as no one had thought to mention that there were mares in foal amongst the horses. It was also a fairly safe assumption that none of them had already acquired their sea-legs.

Some of our floating stables.

As we let go our shore lines it was straight into our first feeding time in our zoo and for our other deck passengers, with an unscheduled and sudden opportunity to get to know ' Judy ' the leopard cub much more personally. Judy was on her way to the Edinburgh Zoological Gardens having apparently reached the age when she could no longer be trusted to act as a pet; from here on she would be capable of behaving like a wild animal. Certainly we found that she had her moments. Her 'cage' was a large wooden crate with a barred opening at the front alongside a vertically sliding door. The sides had horizontal vents at floor level to assist mucking out, but these had been secured for transit purposes.

The instructions indicated she would be expecting a large dish of milk at this time. Problem: introducing a full dish of milk into the cage past the bars. "It'll have to go in through the door" I announced as I removed the fastenings to allow it to be raised, as this too had been secured for transit. "You get ready with the milk and I'll take charge of the door" I added. All seemed to be ready. And so with an admiring group of spectators gathered closely around on deck, I lifted the door, which came up a bit more than I had intended, looked round to see where my shipmate was with the dish of milk, and looked back to find Judy on her way out by a good head and shoulders. At this point I was aware of ramming the door down with one hand while 'persuading' her back with the other, I don't know which of us was more surprised but luckily for me I managed to get her to retreat back inside and succeeded in closing the door.

My lovely friend Judy.

The spectators had vanished in a flash and were only visible peering out from the safety of nearby portholes as we regrouped and tried again, being careful not to open too soon or too much. Not a good start, and from then on I was determined to reach a better understanding with her. Over the next few days I studied my new charge in some detail. Her bright eyes, the brilliant markings on her lovely coat, and the readiness to play, and I was hooked. She was *beautiful*.

The main obstacles to a friendly tussle while cleaning out the cage were her sharp claws and impressive teeth until I found that by grasping her paws firmly you could prevent the claws coming out as she needed to spread her pads to activate them. That brought the teeth in to play until I noticed that she had no back teeth behind her tusks, just gums. And it was possible to get your hands past the tusks to the gum zone where they were safe. I'd solved the problem and from then on I could at least keep her occupied while we carried out the chores.

I never forgot however that she was allowing me to do this, probably because it was fun, and I learned never to try it when she was feeding on raw meat when jungle manners returned with a vengeance, accompanied by 'motor cycle noises' deep in her throat. We stayed good friends until I had to say goodbye in London docks with a final 'handshake' as her cage was hoisted by the crane. However, this failed to convince the dockers that they should get anywhere near her cage, even when offered a bunch of tenners by the Agent. Sadly I never did get to visit her in the Edinburgh Zoological Gardens but feel sure that she at least left the ship a happy leopard.

Our introduction to the monkeys was perhaps less confrontational but ended very definitely, one up to them. They were housed in a vertical bank of small cages which had wire netting fronts which stopped an inch or so above the floor of each cage to allow food to be introduced in trays, and the inevitable mucking out.

My cabin mate decided he would do the honours, and laid out the trays on the top of the cage which was at a convenient height but this required him to stand against the front of the cages. To complete the scene, I should explain that being in the tropics we were all in shorts but not much else, and by chance the legs of his shorts finished level with the opening below the netting of one of the cages. The next moment with a yell he leapt back from the cage, hands covering his manhood.

Monkey business.

The little blighter had reached up inside the leg of his shorts (no doubt in search of nuts) and thought he had found some, albeit rather firmly attached! On the other hand it was hard to believe he wasn't aware of exactly what he was doing.

As we proceeded across the Indian Ocean all seemed to be well until one Sunday afternoon, resting on my bunk, I became aware of shouting and a commotion on deck. The Barking Deer had escaped and was enjoying the freedom of being able to canter from on end of the ship to the other, made possible by the 'flush deck' hull design.

Without wasting time enquiring how it had got out we settled down to the task of re-capture. All attempts to get near it while standing at the fo'c'sle or poop were met with a sudden departure as it went hell for leather down to the other end. Two problems were identified at this stage: one, it was travelling at about 30mph, and two, it had long tapered horns of pitch fork quality which with head down cleared the deck in front of it by some two inches.

Rolling home with our load of animals.

Our first serious attempt to apprehend it relied on a solid wall of humanity stretched across the fore-deck ready and waiting for its next appearance. To our surprise the animal made no attempt to stop or even slow down, which resulted in a mass resort to presence of mind and absence of body as the line parted and re-formed again behind it. At this point the Second Mate from his grandstand position on the bridge could be heard to be offering: 'Five to four the field'.

We were going to have to be more resourceful, and so with big game practices in mind we found a cargo net made of heavy rope with about an eight inch mesh and erected it as a 'fence' across the fore-deck. When ready we signaled to the crew down aft and sure enough the 'dig a dig' could soon be heard as he obligingly cantered forward again.

To our amazement however, he headed straight for the net, and without slackening speed or deviating he passed through as though it wasn't there and certainly appeared not to have even touched it. Our last resort was to hang the net horizontally and drop it onto the deer as it passed beneath. But this was no more of a problem than the fence, but by this time it had had enough and did not stop when reaching the poop.

Stopping to pick him up was never going to be an option to us but I did feel the loss and never learned the truth about how he broke free, but felt it ill behoved me to criticize after my experience with Judy.

For those who missed this tragic performance, there soon came another opportunity to see us demonstrating our skills which had a much more satisfactory outcome for the animal concerned. The subject of our attention this time was 'Sharda' – a grey mare of modest stature who had always been a favourite of mine and I felt we had a special relationship.

Nevertheless facts had to be faced – not only was intake not being matched by output, so to speak, but soon there was no intake either. She was, without doubt, off her grub. I had to admit it, she was *constipated*.

Our notes did acknowledge this possibility, which could apparently be dealt with by putting Epsom Salts in her feed. Unfortunately this addition made the feed no more attractive so we had stalemate, and a suitably laced drink administered from a beer bottle with head in the up position didn't seem to work either as most of it fell out again when we let go.

There was nothing for it: we would have to take advice from our agent in Port Said who promptly engaged the services of an Egyptian vet. By this time we were only hours out of Port Said so we agreed to leave things to him on arrival. Up to now my experience of vets had been; of rather tired men who had been up all night delivering a calf but were nevertheless game to go on to the next emergency. Our vet was an imposing figure resplendent in an immaculate white suit wearing the inevitable Red Fez (made familiar to us by Tommy Cooper). He was a portly figure with dark glasses who maintained a very professional air of detachment.

More to the point however, what was he going to do with Sharda?

"Oh she will be given an enema" he said in a rather bored tone.

"Wow!" said I, "this I must see."

"I fear you do not fully understand" he replied. "You will be doing the enema not me!"

Realising that he meant what he said, I protested: "What makes you think the horse will go along with this? After all it is a bit personal and her back legs still work quite well."

"No, no, she will be unable to kick because one of you will have picked up a foreleg and kept it up for the duration." Before anyone else could speak, I volunteered for the foreleg job, as it seemed to me much the best end to be, and I would be able to try and take her mind off what was happening at the other end.

Sharda ruminating . . .

So with that we got straight on with it, pausing only to get the Mate's OK to take the back off the box. The target area was now open to the sea view which seemed healthier and gave the crew more chance to get out of the way. When the buckets of soapy water, the hand pump, and the appropriate special wooden tube were all to hand I leapt into the front of the box and picked up her left foreleg. At that point I remembered I was only wearing open sandals and my toes felt rather vulnerable, making it doubly important that I didn't let go. Such was my determination to hang on with all my strength, I was able to dismiss the impression that she was getting heavier and heavier while the hectic activity behind me reached the pumping stage, when everything seemed to happen at once, a cheer announced the appearance of success accompanied by a loud clang as a back hoof connected with the half empty bucket.

Sharda having gradually tested me out had decided I could be trusted not to let go, I was now leg four, so she was able to lash out with one hind leg sending bucket and hoses flying, luckily missing the gang who dived for cover. The relief was mutual, and the job was done!

I don't think it permanently damaged our relationship, after all we had stood together in her hour of need, and although it may have been a cruel deception of a kind, she never seemed to hold it against me, at least not once she was eating again.

The final episode in this saga, occurred out of touch with our veterinary consultant and was sadly well beyond our own abilities. 'Blue Champagne' was a thoroughbred race horse of elegant stance but to our surprise was found to be in foal and worse still appeared to be starting a miscarriage in her box. As she flailed around damaging herself quite badly we took the desperate step of opening the front of the box and hauling her out onto the hatch top where I endeavoured to hold her head down to stop her trying to get up. The Mate who was finding things very distressing was asked to go to the medical cupboard and bring the chloroform.

"How much shall I bring?" he asked nervously to which we all shouted as one man:

"Enough to kill a horse!" The humour ended there and once she was subdued, it was only a matter of time before the second mate's 0.45 revolver finished the job while I held her head steady. A sad outcome but it was one which we were quite unable to prevent.

Fortunately that was our last casualty, and all the others survived in good fettle. But the one I really missed most was of course Judy, even though the dockers were unconvinced about her lovely nature.

Chapter Eight

Mantola for a Last Fling

I had now reached a milestone in my sea-going career, at which I would be allowed to take my Second Mate's Certificate (although I had not quite completed the length of sea time required). It would therefore be converted from 'temporary' to 'full' status when the remaining time had been served. So my first priority on arriving back in London was to join a nautical school in London's dockland for a final cramming session followed by the examination.

I should explain that like all Cadets, I had been following a training programme laid down by the Merchant Navy Officers' Training Board with periodic tests, all ably assisted by the other watch-keeping officers on board. To my surprise, before leaving *Salviola* I was congratulated by the Marine Superintendant in Bombay for being awarded a certificate of merit by the Training Board for my efforts, although I had to take his word for it because the Certificate never did catch up with me.

One of the more irksome but essential parts of the examination was having to know by heart Articles 17 to 31 of the Rules for the Prevention of Collision at Sea, in other words the mariners' Highway Code which all seafarers have to follow in International waters. At first I was somewhat taken aback to find that the barmaid of the pub next to the nautical school refused to serve us until we had recited maybe Article 19:

"Where two steam vessels are crossing so as to involve risk of collision the vessel which has the other on her starboard side shall keep out of the way of the other." But we came to thank her for devotion to our cause and have never forgot them.

Waving my newly acquired qualification in front of the Company, they lost no time in finding a suitable ship on which to finish my time. And in October 1948, I was appointed as Fourth Officer on the SS *Mantola*, a cargo / passenger ship plying the East African trade out of London. However I discovered that peacetime service on these ships meant following the same course line, almost 'engraved' on the charts, as they regularly plied back and forth between the same places. Promotion, it seemed, would rely more on filling 'dead men's shoes' than on merit. Inevitably this provoked in my mind, almost a feeling of tram driving, albeit in a rather stately tram.

My 'ticket' at last!

In retrospect, I suppose my first few years at sea had led me to expect new challenges along the way and I was suffering from withdrawal symptoms from the Salvage circus. There was little doubt however that I was reaching the momentous conclusion that maybe (horror of horrors) life at sea was not for me after all. Fortunately this decision was not allowed to interfere with the enjoyment of this voyage, where I had no regular watch to stand but merely did meal reliefs for the others. This meant that I was available for parties in the evenings (as many as four per night). And as Company policy seemed to be definitely to keep the passengers happy, I was determined to do my bit.

On my last trip back home from Bombay I had been charged with delivering one of my fellow cadets to his home in Streatham suffering from advanced DTs (Delirium Tremens). He was unable to hold a fork or spoon steady enough to get food all the way to his mouth, so lived on sandwiches. Drinks were a similar problem, and the little animals that he saw crawling about his person had constantly to be brushed away. This had been brought on by keeping pace with the Second Mate of his last ship downing gin by the bottle on a deadly dull regular run, up and down the Persian Gulf. He really was a wreck and I felt bad about the task, that was, until I discovered he had a delightful young blonde sister who I felt obliged to console or at any rate take her mind off things, in any way I could. This aspect of the situation was certainly much more to my taste, and compensated to some extent for the damage her brother had caused to my enthusiasm for competitive drinking.

Here on the *Mantola* I was finding out for the first time about the Tanganyikan 'Ground Nut Scheme' with which we seemed to be heavily involved, conveying both human and mechanical resources to the nearest ports Lindi and Dar Es Salaam. Unbelievably, the scheme, which was politically inspired from Westminster, involved the reclamation and cultivation of some 150,000 acres of scrubland in Tanganyika for the production of much needed cooking oil processed from ground nuts (peanuts).

SS Mantola © NMM

Talking to those involved, it became obvious that a combination of the highly active wild life – including crocodiles, lions and some pretty wild elephants, plus the odd drought and flash flood – was turning the whole operation into something of a farcical disaster. At one point, we were told, a number of elephant pits were dug, cunningly concealed with branches and dirt. But after the first week, the score was:

Elephants : 0   Tractors : 3

Note: The whole thing was eventually abandoned, by which time the few thousand tons of nuts produced had run up a reported bill of £49 million for the long suffering British taxpayer, and a Plan B sunflower scheme also failed through drought.

But 'ours not to reason why' and we would aim to make the nut farmers' journey out as pleasant as possible. I soon got into passenger ship ways, being as eager as the next man to see the new passenger list and sort out the 'misses' and their cabin numbers. But one particular girl came to our attention as we rounded Gibraltar by paying in to the Purser's safe a large quantity of cash which bore no relation to the limited amount of sterling that could be taken out of the country under the post-war regulations that were in force at the time. It seemed she was on her way to a new life: to join her fiancé in Tanganyika and get married. But it was not long before she had developed the habit of dropping in on us young watch keepers for morning coffee and a chat. Her distinctive and rather piercing cockney voice made her easily detectable when on our nightly rounds we stumbled over one of the blanket-clad pairs of bodies which seemed to favour the dimly lit boat deck.

The temptation to impress on her that we knew where she had spent some part of the previous night was too great. But not content with that, we went on to explain that it was of course our *duty* to know everything that went on in the ship. This news had obviously surprised her but more unfortunately she appears to have actually believed us.

So we were completely taken aback the following morning when she boycotted our group altogether. It was some time before we were able to penetrate the protective screen of anger and resentment. Eventually we got the story, and it was obvious that we had let her down completely – even though the real villain of the piece was in fact a fellow passenger.

"That randy old sod from cabin XX had me pinned against the boat deck rails at one o'clock this morning and I said 'if you don't let me go I'll scream', and he said 'go ahead and scream, no one will hear you', and so I screamed, and if you guys really know it all *where the b******g hell* were you?"

She was a bit too upset to be told that we had been winding her up and that our discoveries were purely by chance So we had to find a reason why we couldn't be there at the time but we promised to try and keep a closer eye on her in the future, although she didn't seem to be dead sure that this was what she wanted either.

None of this did much for my better understanding of women although one fact was inescapable – they were a lot more available at sea than they ever were on land – even the Missionaries' wives (but that's another story).

Local taxis and traders standing by at Lindi.

I suppose that there was a feeling, at least amongst those who were coming out from UK, that after a long period of wartime austerity, they could at last let go and enjoy peacetime cruising with its gargantuan meals and wild parties in exotic surroundings.

No one wanted to be left out and I remember the Second Purser being the subject of a complaint to head office from a mature lady passenger because he had changed his allegiance at one port in favour of a younger model who had just joined us.

"Not the sort of treatment that a long standing loyal passenger has come to expect from your company", she complained.

For my part I managed to make myself really conspicuous by coming to the aid of yet another young passenger who asked if there was somewhere dark where she could open her camera and sort out a troublesome film. We happened to be down on the Promenade Deck where I knew of one cupboard just about large enough for the two of us which opened directly off the outer deck. So in we went to sort it out. I had, of course, overlooked the fact that the Captain and his entourage were about to pass along the deck in the course of making his daily 'rounds' to check the cleanliness, good order and discipline of his proud vessel. As I flung open our cupboard door and we stumbled into the bright sunlight again we all but knocked the 'Old Man' flying. Luckily he was so taken by surprise that he appeared to accept my hasty explanation and the entourage were more amused than shocked. Just another example of the risks we all took to keep the passengers happy.

It was always maintained that you should never pass within half a mile down wind of a B.I. ship or you were likely to become intoxicated on the alcoholic fumes and I'm sure we were no exception. I think this only reinforced my intention to 'swallow the anchor' (as going ashore again was called) at the end of the trip, as being the best way of living to see 35. Yes, it was an amazing job to be getting paid for but I found it worrying that all the mental exercise and exams would be over by my mid twenties leaving nothing but routine. Where would be the challenges that would match those which must surely be awaiting me ashore?

The whole matter was nearly taken out of my hands however when floating in the ship's swimming pool (built on No. 2 hatch whilst at sea) one afternoon after having been unexpectedly relieved of my watch duties by the Old Man. I marvelled how close we seemed to be passing some islands when seen from the pool. In a flash I remembered I had given the quartermaster a course correction to counter leeway we were experiencing, and had not handed this over to the Old Man before leaving the bridge. My feet barely touched the deck until I was standing on the bridge in a pool of water, staring into the face of the Captain whose expression said it all.

"I think you forgot to tell me something, Fourth", he said. Before I had the chance to attempt an explanation, he just said: "Don't do that again", and unbelievably the incident was closed. I could hardly believe my ears having apparently just hazarded the ship. I at least expected to be hung out to dry.

By now I was focussing on my next career, eyeing the concessions available to ex-service personnel, filling in applications and waiting for places to be allocated which would turn me into a Building Surveyor (with all that that promised). After all, I could always go back to sea if I didn't like it, and indeed the Old Man assured me that would be the case as 'the sea was in my blood'.

One thing I never doubted, was how privileged I had been to have served on coal burning steam ships, with their triple expansion engines plying the trade routes and handling their own cargoes by the hook and the net swinging from their own derricks. Coaling at Port Said or Aden was a never-to-be-forgotten experience with coal carried in shallow baskets on the heads of men and women working as 'coolies', who climbed the gangways from the coal barges to throw the coal into the hungry bunkers. On one occasion I discovered a worker had fallen out of line to lie down on the deck behind the hatch coaming. On unwisely investigating, I found to my horror that she had merely paused for a few minutes to have a baby before going back to work still covered from head to foot in coal dust.

How I thought I was ever going to beat all that in my new way of life, I don't know. But as I sat in front of my new boss in his plush office in the City of London a few months later, one home truth slowly penetrated my mood of anticipation and caused me, for the first time, to have a niggling doubt about it all. It seemed that if I worked very long and very hard I could eventually expect to sit back and enjoy a lifestyle such as his. As it happened, he was just about to go off on one of his favourite breaks – *cruising the oceans on a luxury liner*. Hang on a minute. It seems I would be chasing my own tail here, if the rewards for all this new effort would merely put me back where I started. What was I doing?

Discounting this incentive therefore, and bearing in mind my desert Arab friends' contention that there is a limit to how comfortable you can expect to become, it finally hit me that it was job satisfaction that was needing. What's more I would now be able to follow my instincts and interests beyond the confines of the small world of a ship at sea.

I had fulfilled my life-long ambition to go to sea, and was now ready to play my next part, accompanied by memories which would never become dull and would lose nothing in the re-telling.